HT WEIGHT SYMMETRY COMMITMENT MONOGAMY PENIS SIZE SMILES
ONS CHEAP SPERM PRECIOUS EGGS SUCCESSFUL WOMEN YOUNGER MEN
-DECEPTION SEXUAL CONQUEST BIG BALLS WAIST-TO-HIP RATIO EYE COP
Y PROMISCUITY HEIGHT WEIGHT SYMMETRY COMMITMENT MONOGAN
ANCE DESIRE MASTURBATION EXPECTATIONS CHEAP SPERM PRECIOUS
KET GIRL POWER HIGH-STATUS MALE SELF-DECEPTION SEXUAL CONQUES
UMOR BRAIN ACTIVITY SMELL FERTILITY PROMISCUITY HEIGHT WEIGHT
DONNA VS. WHORE UNCONSCIOUS ROMANCE DESIRE MASTURBATION E

INTERNET DATING UNCONSCIOUS ROMANCE DESIRE MASTURBATION E
IOGRAPHIC   GH-STATUS
  DATI   SMELL
NIS SI   CONS
 SUCC   L MA
 BALLS   ALTY
METRY C   ERNET D
ATIONS YOUNGER MEN DEMOGRAPHICS DATING POOL MARRIAGE MARK

Decoding Love

*Why It Takes Twelve Frogs to
Find a Prince and Other Revelations
from the Science of Attraction*

ANDREW TREES

AVERY
A MEMBER OF PENGUIN GROUP (USA) INC.
NEW YORK

Published by the Penguin Group
Penguin Group (USA) Inc., 375 Hudson Street, New York, New York 10014, USA •
Penguin Group (Canada), 90 Eglinton Avenue East, Suite 700, Toronto, Ontario M4P 2Y3,
Canada (a division of Pearson Canada Inc.) • Penguin Books Ltd, 80 Strand,
London WC2R 0RL, England • Penguin Ireland, 25 St Stephen's Green, Dublin 2, Ireland
(a division of Penguin Books Ltd) • Penguin Group (Australia), 250 Camberwell Road,
Camberwell, Victoria 3124, Australia (a division of Pearson Australia Group Pty Ltd) •
Penguin Books India Pvt Ltd, 11 Community Centre, Panchsheel Park, New Delhi–110 017,
India • Penguin Group (NZ), 67 Apollo Drive, Rosedale, North Shore 0632, New Zealand
(a division of Pearson New Zealand Ltd) • Penguin Books (South Africa) (Pty) Ltd,
24 Sturdee Avenue, Rosebank, Johannesburg 2196, South Africa

Penguin Books Ltd, Registered Offices: 80 Strand, London WC2R 0RL, England

Most Avery books are available at special quantity discounts for bulk purchase for sales
promotions, premiums, fund-raising, and educational needs. Special books or book excerpts
also can be created to fit specific needs. For details, write Penguin Group (USA) Inc. Special
Markets, 375 Hudson Street, New York, NY 10014.

Library of Congress Cataloging-in-Publication Data

Trees, Andrew, date.
Decoding love : why it takes twelve frogs to find a prince and
other revelations from the science of attraction / Andrew Trees.
p.   cm.
Includes bibliographical references and index.
ISBN 978-1-58333-331-0
1. Sexual attraction.   2. Dating (Social customs).   I. Title.
HQ23.T74   2009   2008042195
306.73 — dc22

Printed in the United States of America
1   3   5   7   9   10   8   6   4   2

Book design by Lovedog Studio

While the author has made every effort to provide accurate telephone numbers and Internet addresses
at the time of publication, neither the publisher nor the author assumes any responsibility for errors, or
for changes that occur after publication. Further, the publisher does not have any control over and does
not assume any responsibility for author or third-party websites or their content.

To Heesun,

for saving me from having to go on any more first dates

Contents

Introduction

Romance and Its Discontents

RELATIONSHIPS SHOULD BE SO SIMPLE. YOU MEET SOMEONE. You fall in love. If all goes well, that person falls in love with you. And as the fairy tale says, you both live happily ever after. But the reality is rarely so simple. My goal is to explore why that is the case by taking a rational approach to that most irrational of pursuits, the search for love. Imagine Jane Austen's romances rewritten by people like Charles Darwin and Adam Smith, and you will have some idea of what sort of book this is. The simple premise behind *Decoding Love* is that despite our ingrained prejudice, our current model of finding love is deeply flawed, and science can actually provide a great deal of insight into our quest for romance. It will take something we think we know well—how to find love—and reveal that many of our assumptions are wrong.

There are any number of shocking discoveries that researchers have uncovered in recent years. For instance, did you know that women generally make the first move in a bar? That men find women who are ovulating more attractive? That human testicle size is an indication of how promiscuous women are? That what you can put into words about why you like someone often isn't an accurate reflection of why you *really* like that person? That scaring someone can spark as much attraction as seducing him or her? That the number of frogs you must kiss before finding your prince or princess is a dozen? That women who wear a spicy floral fragrance are judged to be twelve pounds lighter than they actually are? That some men have a gene that makes them more promiscuous? That a woman's orgasms have little to do with love and everything to do with a strange body measurement known as symmetricality? Until I started my research, I certainly had no idea.

I realize that the scientific approach is not one that comes naturally to people interested in falling in love, but I believe that is because we are the victims of hundreds of years of stories and novels and plays and poems and movies and television shows about a certain version of love. These stories have hammered into us a collective wisdom about what it means to be in love and how to go about finding that love—or what I call the romantic story line. As soon as you look for it, you realize that it's everywhere. George Orwell's worst nightmare of mind control never achieved anything like the stranglehold that the romantic story line has over all of us. It wouldn't matter so much—we all carry around many mistaken beliefs about life—except that it has become a source of misery to many single people and quite a few couples as well. With a divorce rate hovering near 50 percent, you don't have to be a rocket scientist to see that something has gone seriously awry.

If using science to find love seems crazy, though, imagine how insane our current system would look to an anthropologist from Mars. Our Martian—let's call him Zog—would soon learn that finding a romantic partner is just about the most important thing most of us do. We lavish vast amounts of time and effort and money on the search. But, despite our best efforts, almost half of us will end up divorcing that same person we worked so hard to find. And then we will begin the search all over again. What else could Zog say, except that we are mad for love?

If the extraterrestrial perspective is too far out, let's make a quick comparison between our model of romantic choice and arranged marriages, an approach that runs counter to every aspect of the romantic story line. The divorce rate in this country is close to half, while the divorce rate for arranged marriages is almost zero. Talk about a stark contrast. In our culture, by the time we are teenagers we don't even let our parents choose our clothes, let alone our partners. And we devote huge amounts of energy to the search for love. What is our reward for all of our efforts? Seemingly nothing but heartache, frustration, and failed marriages.

Of course, this comparison is not apples to apples or even apples to oranges (more apples to mangoes, really). There are obviously a host of factors that can influence divorce rates, and Americans have a more tolerant view of divorce than many other countries. But this also tells us something revealing about our romance with romance. The ready acceptance of divorce is itself a sign of how deeply embedded the romantic story line is in our culture, because it depends on one of the deep-seated myths of romantic love, the idea of "the one." When our marriages fall short of the idealized visions many of us have, we often see it as a sign that we have made a mistake, and our current partner is not really "the one." The only cure? Divorce and a renewed search for love. Guided by the enormous expectations of the romantic story line, we dive into relationship after relationship only to have almost all of them end in disappointment. And when they do, we rarely question our approach. We simply start a new search for love.

The good news is that the problem is largely not our fault (at least not personally); instead, our difficulties arise from the romantic story line itself, which has become enshrined as virtually the only arbiter of any relationship. It wasn't always this way. A group of researchers compared different surveys from more than half a century to see how Americans' relationship priorities have changed. As recently as 1939, Americans placed love far lower on the list. For men, it was only fourth, and for women it was fifth (No. 1 for men back then was a dependable character, while women rated emotional maturity as the most important trait—apparently, they're still waiting on that one). But love has been rising steadily ever since, hitting No. 1 for women in 1977 and No. 1 for men in 1984, where it has remained ever since. During this same time, the divorce rate has gained just as steadily. I don't want to claim any simple causality, but it is telling that as love has grown in importance, it has become harder and harder to find and hold on to.

The time has come for us to throw the romantic story line

overboard and fix a cold, clinical eye on love and its attendant complexities—less romance and more science. While we have continued to struggle along without making any discernible progress in our love lives, science has made significant advances. For example, various methods can now predict with more than 90 percent accuracy whether or not a couple will divorce. In other words, hard as this is to believe, when you are sitting at a candlelit dinner and looking into the eyes of the man or woman you think is Mr. or Ms. Right, you are less likely to make the correct decision about marrying that person than someone in a white lab coat using nothing more than a videotape of the encounter or a multiple-choice test.

Decoding Love is my attempt to regain a place at the table for science. We tend to treat finding love as we do making sausage— we don't want to look too closely at what goes into it. Well, this book is going to look closely, and it is not always a pretty story. In fact, some of the insights into relationships are distinctly upsetting, particularly if you cling to lily-white ideas about human nature. But my mission is not to tell us flattering truths about ourselves. It is to try to show us as accurately as possible who we are and why we do the things we do.

There is one enormous hurdle, though, which you must get past if you are going to be open to the information in *Decoding Love*—you must be willing to set aside your own common-sense assumptions and consider with an open mind the research that I am going to present. I know how difficult this is. When I first read much of the material for this book, my own reaction was skeptical, and my wife serves as a continuing reminder of the difficulty of discarding our romantic prejudices. Whenever I came across an interesting study, I would share it with her. She then considered it against her own experience and decided whether she agreed with it or not. If the study failed to align with her experiences, so much the worse for the study. There are various evolutionary reasons for this, but suffice it to say that we are all deeply resistant to impersonal information, especially when it clashes with our own experiences. And it will clash! All of the research in here focuses on the average person's response. Part of what makes us fascinating is that as individuals we all differ from the average in lots of idiosyncratic ways. So, all of this will not apply to all readers, but some of it will apply to each reader.

In the interest of truthful advertising, I should let everyone know that *Decoding Love* has no magic bullet for finding love. I wish it did. If only it were as easy as telling you to put down this book, trundle yourself off to the supermarket, and wait for a mysterious stranger in aisle five looking for lentils. I can promise that the foundation of the book will be based on the latest scholarly advances in a number of different fields to try to understand something at once utterly familiar and deeply mysterious, the relationship between a man and a woman. You may find it hard to believe that some of the things I discuss have been studied—I found it hard to believe myself at times—but rest assured that I am not simply making things up. This is more important than you might think. It turns out that even many relationship "experts" have been winging it much of the time.

In fact, if I am really going to follow the truth in advertising approach, I should tell you that this book is not intended primarily as an advice book. Don't worry. It contains advice along the way. But the deeper interest for me—and I hope for you—is to understand the elusive elements involved when one person is attracted to another and to use that as a window into that which makes us most human. In the end, I hope that this book will provide insight not just into your love life but into your life.

I don't want to present myself as an infallible expert. My research has only deepened my sense that relationships are far more complex than I thought and that when it comes to understanding love, we all know less than we think we do. I have been struck again and again by a simple thought: we are sophisticated and advanced in so many ways, yet when it comes to love, it often seems as if we haven't left the sandbox. *Decoding Love* is my attempt, if not to get us out of that sandbox, then at least to give us a sense of what strange things might be buried within us. After reading it, I hope you will never think about attraction in quite the same way again.

1

The Dating Mind

What I Learned About Dating from Freud—Or at Least from the Subconscious

> *"Man is a credulous animal, and must believe some-thing; in the absence of good grounds for belief, he will be satisfied with bad ones."*
>
> —Bertrand Russell

L ET ME INTRODUCE YOU TO A STRANGER I THINK YOU are going to like—yourself. That's right. I know you've been spending a lot of time with this person. Perhaps you've even grown tired of him or her, and in the great American tradition you hope to exchange your old, boring self for an entirely new one. Before you do that, though, consider the possibility that you scarcely know who you are.

I should be a little more precise when I say that you don't know yourself. I don't mean that you are somehow unaware of what you like and don't like. I mean that your conscious mind is far less aware of the reasons you do things than you think it is. As study after study has revealed, our conscious mind is usually playing catch-up with what is actually going on. It is a little like a busybody who shows up at an accident after it has occurred and then runs around trying to explain to everyone what happened. It tries to come up with explanations that make sense. But those explanations are after the fact and often woefully wrong. As you might imagine, this can have a profound influence on your life, especially your love life.

TOO SEXY FOR MY MIND

Consider sexual desire, something we have all felt so many times that I'm sure everyone reading this book can confidently state the order in which it occurs. For example, a man sees a woman across the room and finds her attractive. His desire leads to arousal, and he heads across the room to talk to her. There are countless variations of this, but in each one we would predict that desire precedes arousal—and we would be wrong! New evidence reveals that arousal precedes desire, that "desire" is merely the conscious label we put on physical sensations that have already begun to occur. Not persuaded? In one study, sexual images were flashed so briefly that they were not consciously seen, and the body still reacted physically to those images, even though the conscious mind remained unaware of them. Simply put, we are not the "deciders" we think we are.

Scientists have even figured out how to manipulate our responses through something psychologists call "priming" (think of priming a pump). In layman's terms, priming is simply using a certain stimulus to influence how people will react. The ability to "prime" individuals has been shown again and again in all sorts of contexts. Do you want to motivate people to compete more when they play an investment game? Leave them alone with a black briefcase. Do you want them to cooperate more? Put a backpack in the room. Do you want people to clean up more after themselves? Pipe in the smell of cleaning fluid. Unsurprisingly, sexual arousal also works to prime people, and not just in the bedroom. In one study, when men were given bras to handle, they suddenly placed a higher value on immediate payoffs over long-term consequences, whether those payoffs involved sex or money or simply eating candy bars.

What does all of this have to do with your love life? It turns out that attraction itself is remarkably susceptible to priming. In a recent study, students were handed either a hot or a cold cup of liquid. Any guesses as to how it influenced the students' perception of the person handing them the coffee? If you guessed that the students judged the person to be cooler or warmer depending on the heat of the beverage, you are beginning to understand the susceptibility of all of us to priming. If you want a real world example, studies also show that putting someone in a nice setting, such as a fancy restaurant, increased how attractive other people found that person.

I thought this sounded a little crazy until I interviewed one woman who had experienced exactly that sort of priming. She went on a date to a nice restaurant, had a wonderful time, and spent all week looking forward to her next date, which ended up being a bit of a letdown. But she chalked it up to an off night and went out with him again, only to be disappointed a second time.

After a few more lackluster dates, she broke it off and didn't see him again. The funny thing is, she never thought that the restaurant itself might have "primed" her until I started discussing my research with her. As I told her about how the setting in which you place someone can alter how that person is viewed, she suddenly interrupted me to say that she had just realized that her change of heart was not caused by the man but by the restaurants. The first one had been so lovely that it had cast a romantic glow over the entire date, including the man in question. Without that setting, though, her feelings for him proved to be tepid at best. In other words, her inconstancy was due not to the fickle nature of attraction but to the fickle nature of priming.

If you want a startling indication of how easily romantic attraction can be spurred with the right priming, try exposing your date to extreme duress, or a little dating technique I like to call shock therapy for love. You see, we don't do a very good job of distinguishing between sexual arousal and arousal related to other emotions, such as fear. So one way to prime an individual for romantic attraction is to scare the hell out of him or her. In one study, male students were brought into a room with a large amount of electrical equipment. The male students were told that the study involved the effect of electrical shocks on learning, but the real purpose was to study the effect of fear on arousal. There were two levels of shock, one that was very painful and another that was mild. An attractive woman was also supposedly taking the shock test, although she was actually part of the experiment. The level of the shock was determined by a coin flip. The experimenter then told the student that he needed to get more information about the student's feelings before administering the shocks, because that could influence the experiment. The male student was sent away to answer a questionnaire, including questions about how much he would like to kiss the woman in the study and how much he would like to ask her out on a date. Being faced with a painful electrical jolt was like Cupid's arrow. The students who were anticipating the painful shocks were significantly more attracted to the woman and had both a greater desire to kiss her and to ask her on a date. In fact, one can simply pretend to go through a painful experience and still elicit a similar reaction. In another study on attraction, male students pretended that a female interrogator was painfully torturing them by putting acid into their eyes (the interrogator actually used water). The students so thoroughly embraced their roles—they screamed and shook with fear—that they later reported they had experienced real fear. The result? They were far more attracted to the female interrogator than male students who only pretended that they were being interrogated in a mild way—a radical twist on the idea of sexual role playing. Perhaps the CIA can get itself off the hook for its new interrogation methods by claiming that they are really dating techniques.

You don't have to hook your date up to a car battery just to spur a little romance. All you need is something at least mildly scary. In a famous study, an attractive young woman waited for men to cross the Capilano Canyon Suspension Bridge in Vancouver. The bridge is only a few feet wide, more than four hundred feet long, and is constructed of wood boards and cables that tilt and sway in the wind. And if you fall off the bridge, you face a 230-foot drop into rocks and shallow water—just the kind of thing to get the heart racing. Once a man crossed the bridge, the woman in the study would walk up to him and tell him that she was doing a project on attractive scenery. She would then ask him some questions. At the end, she would write down her name and phone number and invite the man to call her if he wanted to talk more about the study. As a control group, a similar experiment was run at a much safer bridge nearby. Once the men had been primed for arousal by crossing the suspension bridge, how much more likely were they to call the woman? A lot more likely—*eight times* more likely, in fact. Once we are aroused, whether it is from fear or anger or desire, that arousal will change how we look at someone so that a person we might never have noticed becomes someone we feel a strong attraction to.

Before you go out and start trying to prime some romantic prospect, though, be forewarned. All of these effects were the product of controlled environments in which the participants had no idea they were being primed. Consciously setting out to manipulate another person is more difficult and comes with a big risk—if the person becomes aware of the manipulation, not only does it fail to work, but it tends to backfire. And you can't make someone who isn't attracted to you become attracted just by scaring him or her. Priming will only intensify the feelings that are already present so that if someone finds you unattractive, this type of priming will only make him or her find you even more unattractive.

All of this may seem far-fetched, but my interviews have

turned up countless stories about more idiosyncratic flashpoints that have sparked romantic desire. Call them our personal primers. Something as prosaic as gardening will do. One woman traveled from England for a conference and found herself seated next to a man at breakfast. She never said a word to him. She said that she simply hadn't had her coffee, although he claimed that she seemed to dislike him and scowled at him the entire time. Later, they ended up at a bar with some other people from the conference, where she remained utterly uninterested in his charms—until they started talking about gardening. It was, she said, "as if the lightning bolt struck." Why gardening? It conjured up some of her favorite memories as a child playing in the garden with her sister. Even though she lived in a different country than the man and left the day after meeting him, the two married ten months later. Others recounted similar experiences involving different priming—drinking bourbon, discovering that the person went to the same high school, even a certain perfume (which the man later realized was the same one that his mother wore, leading to a most uncomfortable Oedipal moment). The likelihood is that we all have these personal trigger points, even though we are usually unaware of them. We are all also primed by the romantic story line itself, which teaches us to expect love to occur in a certain manner, although that manner may be a largely false and misleading construction. For instance, we tend to believe that a couple should immediately fall head over heels in love, even though those people are precisely the ones who tend to end up in divorce court (more on that later, in the chapter on marriage).

THE DANGERS OF SELF-PLEASURE

It's not just priming that throws people off. How you frame an issue also has a significant effect. Let's take a relatively simple consumer study of grocery shoppers to illustrate this. Before shopping, one group was asked what was in their wallet—not the amount of cash but simply what else they carried, such as credit cards or coupons. The second group was asked about what they had in their financial portfolios. Neither question has much to do with how most of us typically shop. We don't check our portfolios (if we are lucky enough to have them) before deciding on our grocery list, nor do we worry about whether or not we are carrying a library card. But the researchers found that simply forcing shoppers to focus briefly on their wallets or their portfolios—"framing" their grocery purchases in these different contexts—radically affected their spending. Those thinking about their wallets spent $6.88 on average, but those thinking about their portfolios wound up spending $9.09, an increase of more than 32 percent. Framing is similar to priming, but while priming uses specific cues to influence someone's behavior, framing alters behavior by shifting the context.

As with priming, it turns out that framing relationships can have a profound effect on how the people in those relationships feel about each other. In fact, you can insidiously undermine a relationship just by planting certain ideas about what is normal. That's exactly what Norbert Schwartz did in a study of male college students. Schwartz selected students who were already in a relationship with a steady partner, and he asked them a number of questions about their sex lives. One of the questions was how often the men masturbated, but Schwartz added a sly wrinkle. He used two different scales when he asked the question. One group was given a scale that ranged from more than once a day to less than once a week (the high-frequency scale). The other group was given a scale ranging from more than once a week to never (the low-frequency group, or, in Seinfeldian terms, the masters of their domain). Needless to say, the rigged scales influenced the amount of masturbation the men reported—those on the high-frequency scale reported slightly more than nine episodes a month, while those in the low-frequency group reported slightly more than seven episodes a month—but even with that shift, both groups still fell within the typical range, according to numerous studies of sexual behavior.

The really interesting aspect of the study was how it influenced the men's perception of their relationship. Depending on the scale used, the answers appeared at very different points in the spectrum, even though the actual amount of masturbation was similar. For the high-frequency scale, once or twice a week put them in the middle, which made their answers seem entirely normal and unexceptionable. For the low-frequency scale, though, once or twice a week put them at the high end of the scale, which fostered the impression that they were engaging in an excessive amount of self-flagellation. Planting that one small seed of worry—framing the question so that the students thought that they were masturbating too much—didn't just affect the students' opinions of their sex lives. It affected their entire relationship. In follow-up questionnaires, Schwartz found that these students were plagued with doubts and expressed more dissatisfaction with their relationships. He got a similar result when he manipulated the scales for a question on the frequency of sex between the men and their partners.

All sorts of things in our lives can frame our experiences. For instance, how we experience something has a great deal to do with what sort of experiences we have had in the past. The same experience might seem great if our previous experiences have been awful, or it might seem disappointing if our previous experiences have been fantastic. And it is hard to imagine that this doesn't happen every time you meet a romantic prospect. If your previous partners tended to be wonderful, you will almost definitely undervalue your current one. Or if your experiences have been horrendous, you will probably have an overly positive view of the next person, even if that person is only slightly less horrendous. One woman admitted to a congenital case of this. After enjoying an idyllic college romance, she says her dating life has been a disaster, largely because no one ever seemed to measure up to her rosy memories of her college boyfriend.

If you could manipulate your date's point of comparison, you could make all of this work in your favor—at least according to a recent article in *The Journal of Consumer Research*. In that study, students watched excerpts from the movie *Rosencrantz and Guildenstern Are Dead* and then rated the movie. Afterward, they were allowed to pick one of four free DVDs, one of which was *Rosencrantz and Guildenstern*. But there was a twist. One group of students was offered a bunch of crappy movies (*Lighthouses of Scotland*, anyone?), which made it almost certain that they would choose *Rosencrantz and Guildenstern*. The other

Monet. The other three are captioned cartoons or photos of animals. Which do you choose? Researchers ran precisely this study with college students, and, as you might expect, most people preferred the posters by van Gogh and Monet. No great surprise there. We probably didn't need a study to find that the average college student prefers van Gogh to a kitten playing with a ball of yarn. But that was not the purpose of the study. Researchers were interested in how thinking about that decision might alter it, so they asked half of the people involved to write a short essay explaining what they liked or disliked about the five posters. Afterward, all of the students were allowed to choose one of the posters and then take it home.

A surprising thing happened when students were asked to write the brief essay: after doing that, they preferred the funny posters. When researchers called the students a few weeks later, those same students were less satisfied with their choice than the students who hadn't written essays. So what was it about writing a brief essay that both altered the students' choices and also made them more dissatisfied with those choices? According to the researchers, what we can find words for is not necessarily what is most important. In this case, describing what we find alluring about van Gogh is a lot harder than explaining why we find one poster funnier than another. We think we are coming up with legitimate reasons why we prefer the funny poster, but what we are doing is coming up with reasons we can articulate. The mind, though, works its black magic on our decision so that we believe we are coming up with our deep, heartfelt convictions. That's why the students who wrote about their preferences ended up taking the funny posters home with them. But those written reasons didn't capture their deeper feelings. Once time had passed, and the students had forgotten about their written responses, their unarticulated preferences had a chance to reemerge, explaining why those students were also the ones who felt more dissatisfied.

Maybe you think that posters are too abstract—a representation, rather than the real thing. Well, it turns out that even something as concrete as our taste buds can be flummoxed when we are forced to write about why we like the way something tastes. Two scientists gathered a group of college students and had them sit down and sample five different brands of strawberry jam. Now, one thing that most people will confidently claim is that they know their own taste preferences, so you would think that selecting a favorite jam would be a simple matter. But the study threw in a twist. One group of students was simply asked to choose which jam they liked best. Another group was asked to analyze the reasons behind their choice. When the two groups had their preferences compared to the judgments of expert taste testers, the group who simply tasted and chose came the closest to matching the preferences of the pros.

The question is, why? Shouldn't thinking carefully about a judgment lead to more accurate judgments? Sad as it is to say, the answer is no. Our minds can do worse when forced to "think rationally." In the case of the group asked to provide reasons, the students came up with reasons all right—only those reasons shaped the eventual choices that they made. In other words, they did not think about things in the order that we would suspect. You would imagine that they would taste the jams, pick a favorite, and then try to figure out why it was their favorite. But most of us aren't expert food tasters and aren't trained to think in terms of the qualities of similar foods. So, instead of tasting, choosing, and then analyzing, the students found reasons that they could articulate *and only then* chose jams that would fit with their reasons. And this isn't simply a jam problem—it applies to a variety of food-stuffs. The results were replicated by another study involving chocolate-chip cookies. Actually, it applies to a whole range of things. Whenever people are asked to describe something verbally that is typically not put into words, the process of putting it into words appears to screw up their thinking. When people are forced to describe a color, they later have more difficulty remembering it. When they are forced to describe a face they have been shown, they are less able to recognize that face on subsequent tests.

Of course, we would like to believe that the poster study or the jam study has nothing to teach us about our love lives. While it may be difficult to express exactly what it is that touches us when we look at a great work of art, surely it is a far simpler matter to figure out what it is that we like or dislike about someone. Comforting though such a notion might be, it is wrong. You only need to look at a similar study involving college couples who had recently started dating. Once a week for four weeks, half of the participants had to sit there for an hour and think about their relationship with their partner. The other half thought about an unrelated topic. At the end of each session, both groups had to answer a number of questions about their relationship. As you might expect after learning about the poster study, thinking about the relationship changed how people felt about it. After the first session, the group that had to think about their relationship changed their attitude. Some became more positive, and some became more negative. It would be tempting to point to this and say that, in contrast to the poster study, this reflection helped sharpen people's sense of the relationship. But this was not the case. What the researchers found was that people came up with thoughts about their relationship that had nothing to do with their initial feelings (which were measured before the study began). Did they question those thoughts? No! They changed their feelings to fit with the reasons they had come up with. Although it took them longer, the other half of the participants also had their attitudes changed just as much, simply by answering questions about their relationship. It would be nice to think that these changes occurred because the couples had recently started dating and would understandably be susceptible to changes of heart, but other studies have revealed that this explanation is highly unlikely. Even when married couples and couples who have dated one another for longer periods of time were used, the results were the same.

Another study found that the attitudes of students who had *not* analyzed their relationship with their partners were actually a far better predictor of whether the couple would still be dating several months later than the attitudes of students who had analyzed their relationship. Once again, the study found a disconnect between the things people could articulate and the things they actually felt. As numerous studies have found, when we are forced to analyze our preferences for everything from why we like someone to what food we prefer, the reasons we come up with only rarely have anything to do with the actual reasons. As Alexander Pope warned, a little knowledge is a dangerous thing—a warning that is particularly relevant when it comes to thinking about relationships, which are by their very nature complex and difficult to pin down.

What all this should teach us is a certain humility about our own explanations, particularly if we do not have expertise in a particular area. While an art historian can easily provide an array of sophisticated reasons for the superiority of van Gogh to Dilbert, we non–art historians would be better off simply trusting our intuition. The same holds true for dating. Despite what we may think, the vast majority of us should not consider ourselves experts when it comes to relationships, no matter how great a blow that is to our own egos. We can go wrong in all sorts of ways. If someone fits the profile we think we are supposed to love, we may ignore how we actually feel. If our feelings conflict with some larger belief that we have (I could never love a smoker) or that the culture fosters (love should feel like X), we are likely to ignore our feelings and cling to the belief.

All of this is especially true for women, who are more likely than men to spend time analyzing their relationships. No, I'm not being a chauvinist—studies have shown that women tend to analyze their romantic relationships much more than most men. One woman I interviewed said that when she had gotten serious about finding someone to marry, she and a girlfriend decided to meet for lunch to analyze every new candidate. While the lunches themselves proved enjoyable, they were no help at all when it came to her dating. Forced to state exactly why she should or shouldn't keep seeing someone, she developed increasingly bizarre criteria. She realized things were getting out of hand when she found herself rejecting one man because his ears were too low on his head. She called off the lunches and now tries to curb her need to talk about her dates.

Not only do we do a poor job of figuring out what is important to us about other people, we also don't know ourselves nearly as well as we think. In one study, people were asked to describe how other people viewed them. The average correlation between how people thought they were viewed and how they were actually viewed was a distinctly lackluster 0.40 or so (one would mean perfect correlation, and zero would mean no correlation). So, for example, your view of how giving you are agrees only modestly with how giving your friends think you are—and chances are that your friends are closer to the truth. Other studies have confirmed that the people around us usually have a more accurate picture of our personality than we do, and they are also better at predicting how we will behave.

This doesn't mean that you should rely on these friends to tell you whether or not you should date someone (as we've just seen, there are some serious pitfalls to this approach), but it might not be a bad idea to get their help clarifying what will make you happy in a relationship. You may think that you don't care very much about a certain quality, such as thoughtfulness, but your friend may be able to remind you of the intense frustration you have felt toward everyone who lacks that quality. You may also think that something is desperately important, while your friend can remind you that your last partner had that quality, and it didn't make you any less unhappy. One woman admitted that she almost decided to end the relationship with the man she eventually married until one of her friends chided her for undervaluing the importance of kindness.

YOU WORE RED—NO, I WORE BLUE.
AH, YES, I REMEMBER IT WELL.

Given all of this, it won't come as any great surprise that our memory is not particularly reliable, either, and we are likely to recall events in a number of deeply inaccurate ways that have profound implications for dating. Psychologist Daniel Kahneman, who won a Nobel Prize for his ingenious work on these issues, has discovered that we don't remember an experience with equal intensity throughout. We tend to remember it at its most intense, and we tend to remember the end—what Kahneman has dubbed the "peak-end" rule. In a sign of just how far scientists are willing to go to understand this phenomenon, they did a study of men who underwent colonoscopy exams. Needless to say, having a tube with a camera (thank God for miniaturization!) inserted into your rectum and then being poked and prodded with it for several minutes is not a pleasant experience, and this unpleasantness is itself significant—people will skip regular testing to avoid it, despite the medical benefits. So, if doctors could find a way to make the experience less unpleasant, patients might be more willing to have the procedure. Researchers decided to take advantage of Kahneman's peak-end rule. One group received the standard colonoscopy. The second group also received the standard colonoscopy with one twist (well, not a literal twist—that would be most uncomfortable). After the exam was over, the doctor left the scope in for a brief period of at least twenty seconds. Although still not enjoyable, those final moments were much less distressing than when the scope was being moved around. But the proof is in the, er, pudding. How did the extra time affect the patients? Kahneman's theory held true: the second group remembered the experience as less unpleasant and were more likely to agree to follow-up colonoscopies than the first group.

Your average date is, I hope, much more pleasant than your average colonoscopy, but Kahneman's peak-end rule does provide some easy advice. Try to make sure that the date includes at least one really intense moment of happiness. That will be the moment your date will remember. And whatever you do, end the date on a high note. That will color your date's memory of the entire experience.

BEWARE EXPECTATIONS

Our experience is not only hostage to our slippery memory—it's also powerfully shaped by the expectations we bring with us. Even something as fundamental as how we taste food is remarkably susceptible to manipulation based on our expectations. You only need to look at Brian Wansink's brilliant work as the director of the Cornell University Food and Brand Lab. He has done a number of clever studies at the Spice Box, a laboratory that masquerades as a restaurant. In one experiment, he offered diners a free glass of Cabernet Sauvignon—but with one devious alteration. Although all the diners were given a glass of a wine known as Two-Buck Chuck (the nickname tells you the price), half of them were told that they were being served wine from a new California label, while the other half were told that they were getting a glass of North Dakota's finest. Even though they drank the same wine, their expectations radically shaped their experience. Not only did those diners who thought they were drinking North Dakotan wine rate their wine as tasting bad, they also rated their *food* as worse than the other group. In fact, it altered their entire meal. They ended up eating less and leaving the restaurant sooner.

The power of expectations is so great that it has an almost preternatural ability to become a self-fulfilling prophecy. In one study, after a test was given to all the students in an elementary school, a few students were randomly selected, and the teachers were told that these students had scored so highly on the test that they were sure to excel in the coming year. The parents and the students weren't told about this so that the only difference was in the minds of the teachers. But just that small intervention led to a major difference. By the end of the year, the falsely anointed "exceptional" students showed significantly higher gains in their IQ scores than the other students. In other words, simply leading the teachers to believe that these students were special led those teachers to treat them in a way that ended up making them special.

Experiments have demonstrated the same power of expectations for attraction. In one study, men and women were asked to talk on the phone and get acquainted with an unknown member of the opposite sex. Before the conversation, each man was given a photograph of his supposed partner. The actual photograph was randomly selected from a group that was either attractive or unattractive. The women were not given photographs. Then, the couples spoke on the phone for roughly ten minutes about anything they wanted. Men who had received photos of beautiful women spoke to the women in a way that caused the women to be friendlier and more flirtatious—acting for all intents and purposes as beautiful women, regardless of their actual appearance.

In *The Psychology of Human Conflict*, Edwin Guthrie tells a remarkable story of how one college woman was transformed in real life by a similar experiment. A group of college men chose a shy, socially inept student and decided to treat her as if she were one of the most popular girls at the school. They made sure she was invited to the right parties and always had men asking her to dance and generally acted as if they were lucky to be in her company. Before the school year had ended, her behavior had completely changed. She was more confident and came to believe that she was indeed popular. Even after the men ended their experiment (although without telling her anything about it), she continued to behave with self-assurance. But here is the really amazing part—even the men who "conducted" the experiment came to see her in the same way, so fully had her demeanor been transformed. If only someone would secretly hire the people around us to treat us not as we are but as we wish to be, we might all become the people we aspire to be.

HOW FALLING IN LOVE IS LIKE WINNING THE LOTTERY—BUT NOT IN THE WAY THAT YOU THINK

The point of all of this is not to befuddle you—befuddling though the working of the mind often is. Some people might read this chapter and be tempted to redouble their efforts to impose some sort of rationality on their dating, but I believe that is exactly the wrong response. If anything, all of this information should teach us to trust our intuition more and our conscious mind less. And we should also remember that the tricks our minds play on us are not necessarily a bad thing for our love lives. For example, being in a relationship appears to lessen how attractive we find other people. In one study, male students in a relationship judged unknown women 10 percent less attractive than single men did. Being in a relationship also causes us to exaggerate our partner's good qualities. In another study, 95 percent of people claimed that their partner was above average in appearance, intelligence, warmth, and sense of humor.

Regardless, the vagaries of our minds when it comes to everything from predicting how something will make us feel in the future to remembering how something made us feel in the past should generate a certain amount of skepticism for one of the central claims of the romantic story line—that finding Mr. or Ms. Right will solve all of our problems and make us happy. If you don't believe me, then you need to consider what I like to call the parable of the lottery winner and paraplegic, which reveals that no single thing affects our happiness as much as we think it will. There are numerous studies confirming this, ranging from college students predicting how they would feel if their football team lost to professors predicting how unhappy they would be if they failed to get tenure. But let's go right to the starkest evidence imaginable. I'm going to ask you a simple question: would it bring you more happiness to win the lottery or to become a paraplegic? No doubt, this is an astoundingly easy choice.

Equally astounding, though, is how little the difference is between these choices when you measure people's long-term happiness.

At the moment people first learn their fates, of course, the contrast could not be greater. Lottery winners are ecstatic and often think that all of their problems have been solved, while paraplegics face a level of despair that is difficult for most of us to imagine. But over time, even the best and the worst of events get woven into the fabric of our daily lives. According to more than one study, lottery winners are no happier than people in general. One study compared people who had won anywhere from $50,000 to $1 million in a state lottery with a group of nonwinners. Not only were the winners no happier than the nonwinners, researchers found that many everyday activities, such as watching television or talking with a friend, were no longer as enjoyable for the winners as they were for the nonwinners. What about the paraplegics? Surely, they were significantly unhappier than the average person. But another study revealed that their level of happiness was only slightly lower than it had been before their loss.

No matter how important something is at the moment, we always tend to overestimate how long it will stay with us. Psychologists call this the "durability bias." This holds true even for our relationships. A recent study has shown that people were less upset by breakups than they had predicted they would be. The reason for this is that most of us fail to factor in the positive experiences we will continue to have in the future, regardless of the breakup. Studies have also found that people recover even from bereavement fairly quickly, especially if they can find meaning in the loss. Researchers have discovered that people have a certain set point for happiness, a level that they may stray from briefly when a major event occurs, such as winning the lottery or getting married, but that they generally return to and remain at for most of their lives. Just how quickly do we return to our set points? Usually less than three months. In other words, finding "the one" simply isn't as important as the romantic story line tells us it is.

At the very least, I hope this chapter has made you more aware of the different ways that we are unconsciously influenced, even when it comes to something as fundamental as romantic attraction. That's not to say that any of us are soon going to become the rational creatures we imagine ourselves to be. But at least we can be a little more conscious of the dark recesses of our mind that so often waylay us on the road to love.

2

The Dating Animal

What I Learned About Dating from Darwin

THE FOLLOWING PAGES ARE NOT FOR THE FAINT OF heart. If there is one part of this book that strikes at the very root of the romantic story line, this is it. Based largely on the work of evolutionary psychologists, it shows us not as we wish we were but as we are. What it reveals is the ceaseless struggle between men and women in which dating is a battleground filled with deception and infidelity.

To accept the evolutionary point of view, we must first set aside our natural prejudice that each of us is a unique individual unlike any other. This is undoubtedly true in lots of small ways, but for now we are going to focus on human beings not as individuals but as a species. In truth, the amount of genetic variation among humans is quite small. And although myriad cultures shape us in vastly different ways, evolutionary psychologists look for traits that are shared across cultures, humanity in the aggregate rather than the particular. Evolutionary psychology is predicated on the idea that our thoughts and feelings and behavior—often lumped together under the banner of "human nature"—have been decisively shaped by the challenges our ancestors faced over the last several million years. In fact, if we truly adopt an evolutionary perspective, we are no longer even the main actors in our own stories but simply the puppets of our genes, which are the true units of consequence.

Accepting this premise will be more difficult than you might imagine. When confronted with evolutionary explanations for their actions, most people deny that those explanations have anything to do with their behavior. For example, if a man sleeps with a lot of women, and you suggest that he is doing that in order to increase the number of his offspring, he will point to the fact that he uses condoms and has no intention of impregnating any of the women. On a conscious level, he will be right. Only it doesn't explain why he feels driven to sleep with so many women or why he is willing to expend so much time and energy and money to do that. Below the level of conscious thought lies a deep and instinctual desire in men for a variety of female sexual partners. There is a very good evolutionary reason for that desire—the more women he has sex with, the more opportunities he has to pass along his genes to future generations. And it is this unconscious level that we are interested in.

When you start to look at things from an evolutionary point of view, this kind of disconnect between conscious and unconscious explanations is common. Our culture evolves at a much faster rate than our biology. We are perpetually caught in what you might call an evolutionary time lag. Much of what constitutes our most fundamental drives and instincts developed hundreds of thousands of years ago to deal with the challenges of living in the grassy savanna of Africa. But the fact that our lives no longer resemble those of our prehistoric ancestors doesn't mean that we have also discarded that evolutionary heritage. So, for now, we need to explore the law of the jungle to get a better understanding of just what goes on between men and women.

CHARLES DARWIN—THE WORLD'S FIRST DATING GURU

First, a little background on Charles Darwin, who has had a rough go of it in this country. A substantial portion of Americans still don't believe in evolution, but that's nothing new for Darwin, who has been fighting an uphill battle for quite some time. He first made the case for evolution in *Origin of the Species*—his most famous work—in 1859. But we're interested in a later work of Darwin's, his 1871 book *Descent of Man*, which explains one aspect of evolution: sexual selection.

When we think of Darwin, most of us remember the phrase "the survival of the fittest," or what is known as natural selection. Darwin's theory of sexual selection is a subset of that, what you might call "reproduction of the fittest." To put it in the most basic terms, natural selection has to do with the ability to adapt to the environment, while sexual selection is concerned with how to acquire mates. And it turns out that sexual selection is really the essential element because the key to any animal's success is not simply his or her ability to survive but also his or her ability to pass along genes to future generations. In other words, you can be the fastest male Kudu around, but if you don't know how to make it with a female Kudu, you won't matter from an evolutionary standpoint. If Darwin's original ideas about evolution were slow to gain acceptance, the speed at which sexual selection gained adherents was glacial.

If you are willing to take the Darwinian view seriously, I have some good news, some bad news, and one disappointing truth. First, the good news. You are a spectacular evolutionary success story, representing an unbroken chain of thousands of ancestors who managed not just to survive but to attract a sexual partner and successfully rear a child. So, let me be the first to say, kudos to you!

Now, for the bad news. You are surrounded by people who are every bit as much of an evolutionary success as you are. In fact, you are caught in what biologists have called a Red Queen situation, named for the Red Queen in Lewis Carroll's *Through the Looking Glass*, who says to Alice, "It takes all the running you can do to stay in the same place." And that's the situation all of us find ourselves in now. You see, no matter how well we adapt to our current environment, our competition and our enemies keep adapting as well. We don't have to worry too much about our enemies anymore. Very few of us are likely to be eaten by a lion after all, but we have to worry a great deal about our competition, i.e., other humans, billions strong and growing more numerous every day.

And now for the disappointing truth. Dating—the whole effort to find a lifetime partner with whom to mate—doesn't just seem hard. It is hard. And it's supposed to be hard. That's the necessary outgrowth of a Red Queen situation. Do you ever watch television shows from the 1950s or even the 1980s and find that they seem slow, that the dialogue and plot are crude, the characters shallow and obvious? That's a cultural example of the kind of Red Queen situation I'm discussing. You've come to expect faster pacing and more complex characters. In short, you've become a much more sophisticated consumer of television shows than the previous generation. The problem is that everyone else has become more sophisticated as well, so your growth in understanding doesn't provide a competitive advantage. It only helps you keep pace with the pack. Now, imagine the same scenario for dating. All your hard work in terms of looking good and developing an interesting personality only serves to hold your place. That's why it seems so difficult. The romantic story line blinds us to that fact by serving up the fantasy that finding the right person is as easy as slipping your foot into a glass slipper.

I have an added piece of good news. If you accept Darwin's ideas about sexual selection, then the animal kingdom can shed quite a bit of light on the nature of human relationships. Before I turn to the world of animals, though, I want to add one caveat. I will be discussing biological tendencies, but that is not the same thing as offering moral justifications. For example, just because men have an evolutionary tendency to commit adultery, that does not mean adultery is okay. We are not slaves to our biological urges. We are also products of cultures that establish certain moral and legal codes. But we'll get to cultural explanations in the next chapter.

CHIMPS OR BONOBOS?

So, let's look at man the animal. Our closest relatives are the chimpanzee and the bonobo. The first hominid (not yet a homo sapien but of the same genus) diverged from them roughly six to seven million years ago, which is far more recent than the fifteen to twenty million years biologists once thought separated us. This is actually a very short time in evolutionary terms. At the molecular level, there is only about a 1 percent difference between humans and chimpanzees. We are closer to the chimpanzee than the chimpanzee is to the orangutan, and chimps are not only our closest relative—we are their closest relative as well.

Over the years, biologists have claimed any number of differences between us and primates, only to see them fall by the wayside. The latest—and one of the most sophisticated—is the claim that humans are the only ones to have a theory of mind (the ability to imagine what other people are thinking), but recent experiments have revealed even that order of higher-level thinking to be something that chimpanzees exhibit.

Of course, if we accept that chimps and bonobos are our closest relatives, we are left with one absolutely essential question: are we more like chimps or bonobos? The question carries larger implications than you may realize. Just take the matter of sex. With chimpanzees, power is used to resolve questions about sex. With bonobos, though, sex is used to resolve questions of power. Needless to say, this leads to two very different social orders. With chimpanzees, males dominate, and there is a very strict hierarchy. Alliances are constantly forming and re-forming to try to topple the dominant male chimpanzee who has extensive, although not exclusive, control of sexual access to the females. There is a great deal of posturing and even violence, and it is not uncommon for chimpanzees to kill one another. Think of how violent gangs act in prison, and you have a rough human approximation of a chimpanzee society.

But bonobos are like bizarro chimps. Their social order flips everything on its head. In a bonobo troop, the females dominate. Consequently, male aggression is greatly reduced. And because the males do not have to jockey with one another for sexual access, the males spend a lot less time trying to rise in the hierarchy. If there is a dispute, bonobos generally resolve it using sex and engage in an incredibly diverse array of sexual practices. Picture the most freewheeling sexual commune from the late sixties in America, and you probably have the closest approximation to bonobo society in this country's history. Talk about giving peace a chance! As primatologist Frans de Waal has aptly put it, we are left with a choice between the power hungry and brutal chimp or the peace-loving and erotic bonobo.

This has implications not just for our sex lives but for our political lives as well. According to de Waal, primate evolution suggests that rigid hierarchies came first and that equality only developed much later. Monkeys display a rigid hierarchy, and chimpanzees are somewhere in between monkeys and our own attempts at equality. Lest we think that we Americans have long thrown off any vestiges of a rigidly stratified past, our own voices betray our less egalitarian roots. Below 500 hertz, the voice produces meaningless noise. If you filter out the high-pitched noise, you will hear only a low hum. But it turns out that this noise is a hidden window into the unconscious way we are always monitoring our status within a group. During a conversation between two people, the two voices tend to converge, but the amazing part is that the lower-status person is always the one who makes the largest adjustment toward the pitch of the higher-status person. In a study of guests on *Larry King*, Dan Quayle made the most obvious adjustment of any of King's guests, which should give us some sympathy for the hapless former vice president. Although we are the most sophisticated animals when it comes to communication, with a vast and complicated language, words blind us to these other levels of communication, so much so that a number of studies have shown that animals can better intuit our moods than we can ourselves.

Unfortunately, there is no clear-cut answer about whether humans are more like chimps or bonobos, although recent times provide far more examples of societies organized around violence and hierarchy than they do of societies organized around freewheeling sex. But perhaps the most crucial element of comparison is a key difference. Despite all of our similarities, we diverge from chimps and bonobos in one absolutely essential respect—we are the only ones to form long-term pair bonds. And that difference has enormous ramifications.

WHY WE GAVE UP PARTNER SWAPPING FOR STABILITY

The question is, why? What force caused this behavior in human beings? The answer is quite simple: children. Our babies are born in an almost absurdly helpless condition and remain that way for a long time. Based on studies of modern hunter-gatherer societies (which roughly approximate our original evolutionary environment), children aren't able to produce as much food as they eat until they are about fifteen years old. So, pair-bonding was likely a biological necessity. If women were left to raise the children completely on their own with no help from the father, many fewer children would have survived until adulthood—a far more ruthless calculus than what we find in the romantic story line and one that continues to have more relevance today than we care to admit. Have you ever wondered why evil step-parents are so often at the center of children's fairy tales? It turns out that there is a good reason for this widespread cultural anxiety—a stepchild is *sixty-five times* more likely to be fatally abused than a child living with his or her biological parents.

But pair-bonding didn't just happen overnight. Humans had to evolve in a manner that reinforced the pair-bond, which they did in a number ways. Let's start with sex. The first question is, why even have sex? From a genetic standpoint, it is inefficient, since only 50 percent of your genes are passed to your child. There are plenty of other methods of reproduction—some of them positively mind-boggling—that have evolved in the natural world: multisexual for the swingers out there, female only for the feminists, bisexual for the indecisive, asexual for the squeamish, parthenogenesis (virgin birth) for the Christian, and even a few species in which the sex of an individual animal can change back and forth for the transgendered. We could easily pass along our genes far more effectively if we had gone down the path of asexual reproduction, for example. The problem is that this would have left us vulnerable to parasites, which evolve much faster than we do. How much faster? It took millions of years and roughly 250,000 generations for us to split from chimpanzees and become homo sapiens. For E. coli bacteria to experience a similar number of generations would take only nine years. So, sex was the method humans and other animals evolved to fight back against parasites. Simply put, sex allows for far more genetic variation and helps keep us from succumbing to our various bacterial and viral invaders—another classic Red Queen situation in which our evolving immune systems are working hard, simply not to fall behind the parasites attacking us.

When it comes to sex, men and women can congratulate themselves on being the great endurance athletes of the primate world. No, we can't match chimpanzees or bonobos or many other species in the frequency of our sexual encounters, but we blow away virtually every other primate when it comes to the duration of our coitus. Pygmy chimps clock in at a lightning-fast fifteen seconds, which seems unbelievably short until you consider the common chimpanzee, which manages to get the job done in only seven seconds (although this does not mean that female chimps aren't enjoying themselves. According to one study, female chimps can have an orgasm after only twenty or so thrusts). This is roughly on par with baboons, who take about fifteen pelvic thrusts. Gorillas come in at a leisurely one minute. Meanwhile, the average American couple has barely begun, averaging a full four minutes. We are bested only by the orangutan, which averages about fifteen minutes for copulation, but we'll leave them to one side since they are obviously busy getting it on with one another.

As always when you find this sort of discrepancy in behavior, evolutionary thinking demands an explanation, particularly when there is an obvious downside to increasing the length of copulation. First, during the act, you are vulnerable to attack, and second, the longer you have sex, the more precious energy you are using. The answer lies in the pair-bond. It turns out that sex in humans is much more about developing a bond than it is about procreation. Not that procreation isn't essential. Obviously, that's what all this is about at the end of the day. But that is just an occasional by-product. In fact, if you looked at human sex from the standpoint of efficiency, it's a disaster. Even during their most fertile years, many couples can take months to conceive.

Once you look at sexual activity primarily as a way to strengthen the pair-bond, though, you can begin to make sense of a variety of oddities about human beings. For instance, women have a tipped vagina, which promotes more intimate face-to-face copulation, and large breasts, which are on permanent display and act as a constant advertisement of sexual receptivity totally disconnected from ovulation. In contrast, most female mammals only develop enlarged breasts when they are pregnant. Ethologist Desmond Morris argues that various other features—fleshy earlobes, protruding noses, and everted lips—are also designed to promote face-to-face copulation. Even the loss of body hair was possibly a means of promoting the pair-bond.

Perhaps most important, women developed concealed ovulation, which makes it impossible for men to tell when it's the ideal time to mate. This makes her distinct among primate females, all of which have visible displays of their fertility (think of certain primates in which the females buttocks turn bright red during estrus). Further confounding male efforts to determine the time of peak fertility, women do not limit their sexual activity to the time they are ovulating. These developments likely played a crucial role in cementing her bond with a man. Instead of guarding a woman jealously for a few days during ovulation, the man had to develop a long-term relationship to try to ensure that her offspring would also be his. Anthropologist Helen Fisher has called this the "sex contract" that evolved to secure women the help they needed to raise their children.

CHEAP SPERM AND PRECIOUS EGGS

So, with all of these traits to promote pair-bonds, everything should be great when it comes to the relationship between a man and a woman, right? Unfortunately, no. To understand why, we need to explore the crucial role of two largely unmentioned participants in all of this pair-bonding, the sperm and the egg. It is at their fruitful conjunction that everything happens. But what they do to get there and how their carriers (i.e., men and women) feel about that journey makes all the difference.

It took a while for scientists to realize the significance of this. Although they were busy studying and refining Darwin's arguments, sexual selection didn't receive a lot of attention, particularly when it came to one particular segment of the animal kingdom—human beings. While happy to study the mating rituals of everything from slugs to lemurs, scientists proved reluctant to put humans under the microscope, albeit with a few high-profile exceptions such as Alfred Kinsey. That all began to change in 1972 when Robert Trivers published an essay entitled "Parental investment and sexual selection." Despite the rather pedestrian title, that essay is possibly the single-most influential piece of evolutionary theory to come along since Darwin's original concept of sexual selection. What Trivers discovered was no less than the key to sexual selection, the engine, as it were, that made the whole thing run. That engine was parental investment.

Trivers's revolutionary insight was simple. The investment a parent makes in his or her offspring has a huge influence on how that parent will approach mating. The more investment a parent makes, the more selective that parent will be in choosing a mate. The less investment a parent makes, the more sexual competition there will be to attract a mate. Think of the many men who often crowd around an attractive woman at a bar, and you have a pretty good picture of this dynamic at work. Which brings us back to the sperm and the egg. You see, sperm are cheap. The average man's ejaculate contains hundreds of millions of the little buggers (over his lifetime, he will produce two trillion). And although he has nowhere near the sexual ardor of a ram or even a chimpanzee, a young, healthy man can have sex several times a day. On top of all that, if the man is more interested in being a cad than a dad, he can walk away after planting his seed and never lift another finger, so his parental investment is potentially miniscule.

If a man could have sex with an unlimited number of women and conceive with all of them, he could theoretically father hundreds of children in one year, and some famous historical figures have indefatigably attempted to do just that. According to historical records, Moulay Ismael the Bloodthirsty, the emperor of Morocco from 1672 to 1727, fathered 888 children. Recent DNA evidence suggests that Genghis Khan might have fathered an even larger number, and according to research, a mere nineteen male lineages have played the dominant role in populating the world, a remarkable example of the multiplying power of sexual selection for successful males.

Now, consider the woman and her egg, which is a very precious commodity indeed. A woman ovulates once a month, and once she is pregnant, she must carry that child inside of her for nine months. Even after she has the baby, she will have to care for it, and she is unlikely to get pregnant again right away because breast-feeding makes it more difficult to conceive. Over the course of her lifetime, the typical woman will have approximately four hundred to five hundred ovulations. Compare that to the trillions of sperm men will produce over the course of their lifetime (of course, the egg is 85,000 times larger than an individual sperm). Let's assume that she manages to have one baby a year during all of her fertile years. It's possible she could crack twenty. The record is an astounding sixty-nine, which an eighteenth-century Russian achieved by repeatedly having twins (although this figure is possibly apocryphal). Even that extreme number—any woman who has been pregnant will shudder at the thought—pales in comparison to the number of children a man can father, even if he isn't Ismael the Bloodthirsty. If you are still unconvinced, anthropological evidence also confirms that cheap sperm–precious egg distinction. Seventy percent of human societies involve a payment between the two families.

Any guesses as to what percentage of those require a payment to the bride's family? Ninety-six percent!

Trivers's brilliant insight was to realize the enormous ramifications of this simple difference. For a man, the ideal approach from an evolutionary standpoint—passing along his genes to as many children as possible—is to sleep with as many women as possible. And he shouldn't worry too much about the quality of those women. Ugly women, pretty women, women with no teeth, women who can't spell unilateral—it doesn't matter. Having sex with them costs him very little effort, and all of them provide an opportunity to pass along his DNA. For a woman, though, the ideal approach is to be as selective as possible. With so few opportunities in a lifetime, she wants to ensure that she gets quality genetic material from the father. So, for her, it makes a great deal of difference whether the father is a bright, attractive, funny guy who likes to read Jane Austen or a slack-jawed, humorless oaf who mistreats his dog. Hence, the battle of the sexes—a constant war between men who want to seduce with as little work as possible and women who want to resist until they are sure that the potential father is genetically superior and committed to help. As one research team writes, evolution favors males who are "aggressive sexual advertisers" and females who are "coy, comparison shoppers."

Ah, but wait! We have left out one crucial wrinkle: pair-bonding. In our case, the legal bond between man and wife, which changes the calculus considerably. With marriage, a man is tied to a woman for life. With divorce rates running at almost 50 percent, this isn't really the case, but for theoretical purposes we'll take the "until death do us part" seriously. So what happens to our Lothario under those conditions? It turns out that men become much more choosy as well—at least when it comes to long-term relationships (for short-term ones, most men are still pretty much willing to sleep with anyone). But that doesn't undo all the evolutionary hardwiring related to the sperm and the egg. Even with the legal bond of marriage, men and women still find ample scope to express their natural inclinations: men as the promiscuous sperm producers and women as the precious egg holders. What this means is that conflict is built into the relationship between men and women, and pair-bonding is our attempt to contain that conflict.

Of course, Trivers's theory should come as welcome news to any women currently on the dating scene, because it means that women are firmly in control when it comes to the courtship phase of mating. Harvard anthropologist Irven Devore has even called males "a vast breeding experiment run by women." This goes a long way toward explaining why men (particularly low-status males) have a lower life expectancy—they have to take more risks in order to pass along their genes. Women are probably reading this and thinking to themselves that all this Darwinian theorizing is great, but they don't feel like they have much control at all. And it's true that there are some mitigating factors. Because marriage at least theoretically implies a lifetime commitment, men are also choosy. In addition, demographics and culture can undermine female ascendancy. If women vastly outnumber men, for example, men become the scarce and precious commodity. So, in order to see the underlying control that women exert, I ask you to imagine a simple way that women could change the rules of American dating and marriage: they could refuse to have sex until they were married. No more one-night stands or even any long-term cohabitations. If this happened, all female complaints about men refusing to commit would instantly disappear. While many men are happy to date a woman for years at a time if they can still have sex, they would not be willing to do so if those relationships remained entirely chaste.

WHAT HAPPENS WHEN CHEAP SPERM ARE ON THE PROWL

Since Trivers's revolutionary essay, study after study has demonstrated the significance of the sperm/egg distinction for human behavior (and all other creatures for that matter). Let's start with sex. Given Trivers's theory, you would expect to find extremely different attitudes about sex, and that is exactly what researchers have discovered. For any squeamish women reading this book who would like to believe that men are not the appalling sexual predators that they sometimes appear to be, I suggest that you skip the next few pages.

Simply put, men have a much lower threshold for having sex. If you don't believe me, let's try a little experiment. If you are an attractive woman, walk up to a man on the street and ask him if he wants to have sex with you. Chances are he will say yes. How do I know? Researchers conducted a study of exactly this question. An attractive woman approached a man on a college campus and asked him one of three questions:

1. Would you go out on a date tonight?
2. Would you go back to my apartment with me?
3. Would you have sex with me?

Fifty percent of the men said they would go out on a date that night, which might seem somewhat low given what I have just said about parental investment theory. But remember that a date takes a certain amount of time and money with no promise of any sexual activity. Notice what happens to the numbers for the next two questions. Sixty-nine percent of men were willing to go back to the woman's apartment, and a whopping 75 percent were willing to have sex with the woman (and that last number is probably low—the study noted that men who declined to sleep with the woman were usually apologetic and would often ask for a rain check or offer a reason, such as having a fiancée). Researchers then had an attractive man approach women and ask them the same three questions. When it comes to a date, women are the same as the men, accepting 50 percent of the time. From there, though, the disparity could not be starker. Only 6 percent of women were willing to go back to the man's apartment, and not a single woman was willing to have sex with the man.

I know some of the women reading this book are already thinking that the study isn't valid because there is a fear factor for women accepting invitations from strangers that men don't have to worry about. Well, the researchers realized the same thing and conducted a second study. This time, the men and women were contacted by a close personal friend who vouched for the stranger's character. Then the friends asked one of two questions:

1. Will you go on a date with the stranger?
2. Will you go to bed with the stranger?

Under this scenario, 91 percent of women and 96 percent of men were willing to go on a date — again fairly similar. But only 5 percent of women were willing to sleep with the stranger, while fully half of the men were willing to do precisely that (sight unseen!). All of this is exactly what evolutionary theory would predict. If women are choosier in general, they should be particularly choosy when it comes to a one-night stand.

A whole slew of different statistics confirms this sexual difference between men and women. According to a University of Chicago survey, 54 percent of men think about sex once a day, while only 19 percent of women do, and 40 percent of men masturbate once a week, while only 10 percent of women do. According to another study, 85 percent of twenty- to thirty-year-old men think about sex every fifty-two seconds (which makes you wonder how men manage to accomplish anything), while women think about it once a day unless they are ovulating, when that number rises to three or four times a day. The numbers vary from study to study, but in every single one men think about sex much more than women do.

Men also show a much stronger desire for sexual variety. In one study, college students were asked how many sexual partners they would like to have over various time intervals. Over the next year, women said they would prefer on average to have one sexual partner, while men wanted six. Over three years, women wanted two sexual partners, compared to ten for men. And over a lifetime, the average woman wanted four or five, while the average man wanted eighteen.

This desire for variety is so extreme in men that it can lead to some bizarre behavior. In 1995, Hugh Grant was dating supermodel Elizabeth Hurley, and he still felt the need to solicit oral sex with a prostitute, although his subsequent arrest had no effect on his film career (which suggests that most Hollywood moguls must have an instinctive sympathy for the occasional need to solicit a blow job). There are countless recent examples of men, ranging from Bill Clinton to Eliot Spitzer, taking mind-boggling risks for sexual variety that are almost impossible to explain according to any sort of rational calculation. I think only evolutionary psychology has a satisfying answer, which is that some deep, instinctual drive created by thousands of generations of evolution—in this case, a man's greater desire for sexual variety—was guiding their behavior. Even the clichéd idea of a man's midlife crisis is an expression of this evolutionary urge. According to new research, a man suffers from a midlife crisis not because he is getting older but because his wife is. By coming to the end of her reproductive life, she ignites a deep-seated desire in him to attract a younger, reproductively active woman.

Perhaps the best indicator of differences in attitudes toward sex comes from a study of sexual fantasies by Donald Symons and Bruce Ellis, which explored what each sex dreamed about when they were freed from the usual societal constraints. Both men and women reported having and enjoying fantasies about sex, but the content of those fantasies was completely different. Men fantasized much more often and were much more explicit and more visual in their fantasies. Women, on the other hand, were more likely to include context and feelings, and they experienced emotional arousal (men's fantasies turned more on physical arousal). The women's fantasies were also more likely to contain affection and commitment. Perhaps the starkest difference, though, was in how they imagined their partners in the fantasies. Women were much more likely to include a familiar partner, and when it came to the number of different partners, men left women in the dust. Thirty-seven percent of the men reported that they had fantasized about more than one hundred different people, a threshold achieved by only 8 percent of women. A good proxy of these differences can be found in the kind of erotica that both sexes choose. Pornography—with its explicit visual content and large number of women to choose from—is almost entirely directed at men. Romance novels— with their emphasis on emotional connections and on the relationship between one man and one woman—are almost entirely directed at women.

SEX ON THE BRAIN

It's not just that men have a much greater willingness to have sex or that they seek a much wider variety of sexual partners. Their minds are also biased to perceive sexual interest from women when there may in fact be none. One of my favorite headlines from *The Onion* is, "Area Man Going to Go Ahead and Consider That a Date." Any woman who has had a friendly conversation with a man only to have that man later accuse her of leading him on will know what *The Onion* is talking about. In a number of studies, men consistently interpreted actions on the part of women (such as smiling) as an indication of sexual interest. You can find this quick trigger interpretation even in mundane encounters. In another study, men and women listened to various taped conversations. Some of them were erotic, but many of them were routine. Although nearly all the participants became aroused during the erotic conversations, some of the men also became aroused during the regular conversations. And not only did they become aroused—their response was stronger than the female response to the erotic conversations. It's enough to make a woman hesitant to offer up a neutral hello in conversation, for fear of sending men into a sexual frenzy.

With this in mind, women should keep a wary eye on their male friends. Remember the debate from *When Harry Met Sally* about whether or not men and women could be friends? Well, science has likely found an answer—they can't. Or at least men can't. According to the work of evolutionary psychologist April Bleske, men are twice as sexually attracted to their opposite-sex friends as women, and they consider potential sexual encounters with opposite-sex friends as 100 percent more beneficial. They also overestimate how attracted their female friends are to them. Again, this bias makes perfect sense from a Darwinian perspective. The male brain is not designed to maximize accuracy but to maximize mating opportunities. It's in the man's evolutionary self-interest to see more sexual interest than may actually be there. The downside is only social embarrassment. The upside is the possibility of another opportunity to pass along his genes. In this case, the male bias is not a design flaw but a distinct advantage. In fact, the more intelligent the man, the more likely he is to exhibit what one researcher has called the "she wants me" bias. In one study, men were asked to predict how women would respond to a personal ad soliciting no-strings-attached sex. The most intelligent men wildly overestimated how interested women would be. Revealing again how women are wired in fundamentally different ways than men, the most intelligent women show a very different sort of bias—they assume that a man will be far more distressed by a partner's sexual affair than is actually the case.

PROMISCUITY, THY NAME IS MAN . . . AND WOMAN

Of course, these fundamentally different attitudes toward sex set the stage for an enormous amount of conflict. Given men's desire for a greater number of sexual partners and a social system built around marriage and monogamy, you would expect a fair amount of infidelity, and that's exactly what we do find. David Buss, a leading researcher of evolutionary psychology, has estimated that 30–50 percent of American men have at least one affair over the course of their marriage. Even worse, it does not appear that the state of a man's marriage has much to do with whether or not he is unfaithful. According to a survey, 56 percent of men involved in an affair still described their marriage as "very happy," which is probably the most distressing marital statistic I have ever come across. Before women storm off in a huff and decide to foreswear men altogether, though, they should know that they lag only slightly behind men. Buss estimates that 20–40 percent of American women will also have one affair during their marriage. Another researcher has estimated that the chances of at least one partner being unfaithful may be as high as 76 percent! As you can see, the estimates for the actual amount of adultery vary widely. Apparently, we not only like to cheat on one another, we also like to cheat on studies about adultery.

Women's affairs do differ from men's. According to another survey, most women who had affairs said that they were "very unhappy" in their marriages. Women were also much more likely to form emotional commitments. While 44 percent of the men in one study claimed that they had little or no emotional involvement with their affair partner, only 11 percent of women felt no emotional investment.

These affairs are not simply matters of the bedroom but matters of the birthing room as well. Using a number of studies, scientists have estimated that roughly 10 percent of children are not fathered by their legal father. For obvious reasons, this question has not been studied in any systematic way, and other studies have produced numbers ranging from 5–30 percent. All of this has led one researcher to claim that adultery has been grossly underemphasized as a factor in human evolution.

Of course, when compared to the animal kingdom, we aren't doing too badly because studies have revealed that even in the wild there is a great deal more cheating going on than anyone had imagined. Very few mammals are monogamous. One type of ape, the gibbon, was thought to be monogamous, but once scientists developed DNA testing, they found that gibbons also cheated on their partners. Many bird species form couples, which were once held up for admiration as exemplars of lifelong monogamy, but further research has shot down that heartwarming story. After using DNA testing for the birds, researchers discovered that roughly 30 percent of the offspring were not sired by the ostensible "father." In some bird species, the number of offspring who were not sired by the "lifelong partner" reached as high as 76 percent. Even birds apparently covet thy neighbor's wife. Scientists now believe that monogamy among birds is not due to any sort of romantic bond but is the result of the male's attempt (often futile) to protect his paternity rights by guarding the female.

These paternity numbers came as a shock to most researchers. Although scientists have long thought that males are eager to spread their seed, they assumed that the role of the female was almost entirely passive. One researcher even claimed that copulation was "essentially a service or favor that women render to men." The fact that females (including women) were also promiscuous came as a major revelation (that this was a revelation says a great deal about the power of our cultural biases to shape our thinking). We know why men are interested in multiplying sexual partners. Think back to the sperm and the egg. Sperm is cheap, and sleeping around increases the chances that the man can pass along his genes. But why are women also sleeping around? The egg is the precious resource, and the number of children a woman can produce is relatively small.

Ah, but the woman has her own genetic desires. She wants to find a good provider who will help her raise her children, but she also wants the best genes possible. And the two go together far less than you might think. A woman might only be able to get a man of middling rank to marry her, but if she is willing to have a one-night stand with no strings attached, she will be able to have sex with a much more attractive, successful man. By cheating on her husband, the woman can have her cake and eat it, too—she gets a husband who is a good provider and also gets the best possible genes for her child.

BATTLE OF THE SEXUAL GAMETES?

I know this sounds far-fetched. Women don't cheat on their husbands with the express thought of getting their hands on better genetic code. Remember, though, that much of what we are talking about in this chapter occurs below the level of conscious thought. The skeptical among you might use this as a chance to dismiss what I'm saying, but you don't have to take my word for it. You simply have to look at the human body itself. And what does it show? A constantly evolving arms race between men and women—only in this case the battle is waged not by us but by our proxies, our sperm and our eggs. What we have is a classic Red Queen contest where each side wants to gain an advantage. The man would like to impregnate every woman he sleeps with, while the woman would like to be able to choose who fathers her child. She might find a man who is good enough to marry but still want top-notch sperm from someone on the side. If what I'm saying is true, you would expect both men and women to develop measures to increase their chances. We've already seen one very successful strategy of women to thwart a man's ability to police her fertility: concealed ovulation. But it doesn't stop with concealed ovulation. Both men and women have developed a host of subtle and shocking measures to increase their chances of genetic success. These measures are both a sign of how deeply we have been shaped by sexual selection and also a disturbing indication of how we are unwitting pawns in a largely invisible genetic struggle. In short, we are a long way from the romantic story line now.

The clearest evidence of this battle comes from an ingenious study of the fruit fly, published by William Rice in 1996. What Rice did was allow male fruit flies—but not the females they were breeding with—to evolve for forty-one generations. This was a boon for the males. They gradually developed much more effective sperm so that when they mated with a female who had already mated with another of Rice's evolved males, they were much more likely to impregnate her. The reason for their success? Much more toxic sperm, which basically killed off the rival sperm. That trait came with a cost, though, and the cost reveals quite clearly that sexual evolution is not a matter of both sexes cooperating—it's usually a case of one sex developing a quality that is actually antagonistic to the other sex. Just how antagonistic? The sperm had grown so toxic that if a female fruit fly had sex with enough of these evolved males, the sperm had a good chance of killing her—talk about a toxic bachelor! Luckily, human sperm remain far from lethal, but an equally fierce competition is being waged every day between our sperm and our eggs.

So, let's wade right in and start with one of the more controversial aspects of human sexuality—female orgasm. There is still a fairly vigorous debate about whether or not there is any point to a female orgasm. Although feminists might feel that this is some sort of chauvinistic joke masquerading as science, the subject of female orgasm is a serious issue. The reason for a male orgasm is obvious—the release of sperm. And that also helps explain the almost clocklike regularity of male orgasm (as well as the tendency of some men to ejaculate prematurely—there are many positive benefits to the man coming as quickly as possible, and the downside is borne by women). But women ovulate once a month and can be impregnated without any orgasm, leaving scientists to ponder why a woman needs to have an orgasm at all.

Although by no means settled, there is one school of thought I find persuasive. It appears that female orgasm might function as a highly sensitive sexual selection device—and one that sticks a dagger into the heart of the romantic story line. Researchers conducted a study of when women had orgasms. The surprising finding was that the level of a woman's romantic attachment did not increase the frequency of her orgasm, nor did it depend on the man's sexual skill. That's right. Despite hundreds of books on how to be a better lover, women's orgasms have little to do with a man's abilities or even the love the woman has for a man. What did increase the likelihood of female orgasm? How symmetrical a woman's partner was—in other words, how much a man's left and right sides mirrored each other. I know that sounds preposterous, but symmetricality is actually a pretty good indicator of health, i.e., genetic fitness. The more disease and illness, the less symmetrical someone tends to be (studies have also found that less symmetrical men tend to have lower IQs). Think Quasimodo, and you will have an extreme version of someone who is asymmetrical. And researchers have found that women orgasm more with symmetrical men. Simply put, female orgasms appear to be largely predicated on a subconscious evaluation of a man's genetic merit.

So what does all that have to do with the orgasm as a sexual selection device? Robin Baker and Mark Ellis studied whether or not a woman's orgasm had an effect on the amount of sperm her body retained, and what they found was that a woman's orgasm has an enormous effect. If a woman doesn't orgasm or has an orgasm more than a minute before the man ejaculates, she retains very little of the sperm. But if she has an orgasm less than a minute before he does or up to forty-five minutes afterward, she retains most of the sperm, which vastly increases the chances that her egg will be fertilized (they measured the "flowback"— the amount of ejaculate discharged from the vagina shortly after sex—from more than three hundred copulations, by having the women squat over a beaker). So, a man who can make a woman orgasm (i.e., a symmetrical man) has a much better chance of impregnating a woman. Scientists call this sort of hidden mechanism that helps a woman's body choose sperm from a particular male "cryptic female choice."

All of this takes an even more disturbing turn when you bring infidelity into the equation. Remember the theory that wives are unfaithful in order to go after genetically superior sperm? It appears that the female orgasm may be actively aiding in this strategy. Another study revealed that wives who were having affairs tended to have adulterous sex at their most fertile times and that 70 percent of those copulations resulted in an orgasm (as opposed to only 40 percent of the copulations with their husbands). In other words, not only were unfaithful wives more likely to have sex with their lovers during their most fertile period, they were also more likely to orgasm and to retain a larger amount of sperm. When the researchers did the math, they discovered that a wife could have sex twice as often with her husband as with her lover but still be more likely to conceive with her lover (studies have also shown that women with regular partners fake orgasms more often, likely as a way of diverting suspicion about their fidelity).

How likely is it that this sort of hidden sexual selection occurs? A lot more likely than any of us would like to believe. In one study, researchers estimated that 4–12 percent of children born in Great Britain were conceived in an environment of sperm competition, which basically means that sperm from multiple men were in the woman's vaginal tract at the same time and competing to fertilize the same egg. The same study suggested that the majority of men and women in Western societies have at one time or another engaged in sperm competition. Another recent survey found that one in eight female respondents had sex with two or more men in a twenty-four period.

Appalling as this method of "cryptic female choice" may be from a man's point of view, it makes perfect sense from the woman's point of view. Studies have shown that symmetrical men cheat more often, so the woman is better off going after good genes from the symmetrical man but finding a good provider somewhere else. What all this means is that, far from being some useless evolutionary by-product, the female orgasm is quite possibly a remarkably sophisticated mechanism for the selection of superior sperm.

There are even a few researchers who have proposed the controversial theory that a man's sperm are designed to war with other sperm. According to this view, fewer than 1 percent of a man's sperm are designed to fertilize the egg. The rest are a kind of army used to prevent another man's sperm from fertilizing the egg. Most now consider this idea far-fetched, but it is safe to say that sperm and eggs are locked in an evolutionary arms race and will likely remain that way indefinitely.

Males are not defenseless in this high-stakes genetic game. One strategy they have evolved is virtually relentless copulation to ensure paternity. Some mammals have even developed copulatory plugs—their ejaculate contains a substance that literally blocks the sperm of rival males. While human males don't have anything quite so medieval sounding, they have their own "weapons." One recent study has theorized that the ridged glans on a man's penis is designed to scoop out a competitor's semen, and the last part of a man's ejaculate contains a natural spermicide, a kind of before-and-after protection system against female promiscuity. Researchers have also done a study comparing the ejaculates of men who spent 100 percent of their time with their wives with men who spent less than 5 percent of their time with their wives. The result? Men who have been absent ejaculate with almost twice as much sperm—712 million versus only 389 million. Also, human semen contains prostaglandin, a hormone that can cause uterine contractions and thus undermine the selectivity of the female orgasm. This suggests that men also have some very finely honed evolutionary devices to try to ensure the paternity of their offspring.

Even on the level of genetic code, men and women are locked in conflict, as Matt Ridley has shown in his fascinating book *Genome.* At some point in the past, humans switched from the reptilian method of determining sex by the temperature of the egg to a genetic method, which allowed for specialized sex genes to develop. But this is a volatile situation because what is good for one gene can be bad for another gene. For example, the ability to seduce is a great gene for a Y chromosome, but the ability to resist seduction is good for the X chromosome. If one chromosome could strip a quality from another chromosome, that would be a huge advantage for one sex. The problem is that the genetic battle between X and Y is not really a fair fight, because the X chromosome can dominate the Y chromosome. Women have an XX chromosome, and men have an XY. For every one chance a Y chromosome has at undermining something in the X chromosome, the X chromosome has three shots to do the same thing. In this instance, the sexual arms race is a slaughter, and the Y chromosome has done the only sensible thing—run away and hide. To do that effectively, it has become small, very small. While the X chromosome has more than one thousand active genes, the Y chromosome has only twenty-five. Over time, it has basically shut down all but a few essential ones. This gives the X chromosome very few targets to go after and helps make sure that the genetic arms race doesn't end in complete surrender. Little did you know that the struggle to find Mr. or Ms. Right was being fought even on the genetic level of individual chromosomes, and that a woman's X and a man's Y are busy trying to stick it to each other.

DATING AND DECEPTION

Given this ceaseless battle on both the human and genetic level, relationships are rampant breeding grounds for deception. Part of the problem is that modern society provides far more opportunities to lie. In our ancestral environment, social groups were smaller, and those who lied would gain a reputation for dishonesty. But in today's environment, especially in cities or other highly populated areas, there is a much smaller chance of being caught. Internet dating has only increased the problem. Not surprisingly, men and women in relationships lie to each other all the time. In a 1990 study of college students, researchers found that 85 percent of the participants had lied to a partner about a past relationship or an indiscretion. Another study revealed that dating couples lied to each other in about one-third of their interactions. The numbers do improve for married couples, who lied in only 10 percent of their conversations, although the survey found that married couples saved their biggest lies for their partners. Your spouse is probably telling the truth about whether or not she likes your new tie but is possibly lying about whether or not she slept with the mailman. While men are more dishonest than women, they are at least more honest about their dishonesty, giving more accurate estimates of how much they lie than women do. And those are just the lies that we openly acknowledge. The most successful lies are those that we do not even know we are telling, and studies have shown that we are quite good at lying to ourselves about many things having to do with mating, such as how committed we think we are to someone when we are trying to get him or her into bed.

The deception occurs along predictable lines. Given a culture that frowns on female promiscuity—a man's greatest fear in any relationship revolves around questions of fidelity and paternity—women quite commonly lie about their sex lives. This helps explain why sexual surveys always show a gross disparity between the number of partners men and women have had (the other cause is that men exaggerate the number of their partners). Researchers found that if they hooked female college students up to a fake lie detector and then asked them about the number of sexual partners they had, women suddenly reported almost twice as many as the women who were not hooked up to the bogus lie detector. For men, there is a quick and easy way to try to get a sense of a woman's fidelity—if they can get her to divulge her sexual fantasies. One researcher has found that women who have more sexual fantasies about other men are also more likely to be unfaithful. Women also tend to lie about their bodily appearance, although they probably prefer to consider things like padded bras and control-top panty hose enhancements, rather than outright deceptions.

Women I interviewed frequently admitted that they did not tell men the truth about their sexual pasts. To give one example, an attractive woman in her late twenties was incredibly self-confident about her sexuality and had no problem sleeping with a man for her own pleasure and then never seeing him again. She had already racked up more than thirty partners, and she used to proclaim that fact proudly to the men she was dating—until she realized that they couldn't handle the information. Some immediately freaked out. Others went off to sulk. In almost every case, it hurt the relationship and sometimes even ended it. Now when she is asked, she always answers that she has slept with six men, which seems to strike the perfect balance between being a prude and being a slut. Another woman said that men she had dated were often afraid to ask because they didn't want to break the illusion that she had never been with other men, which was an illusion she was happy to allow them to cling to.

While men's greatest concerns center on a woman's potential promiscuity, women get more angry when a man has lied about his income or status or when he has exaggerated his feelings in order to have sex, and studies confirm that men lie more about their resources and their level of commitment as well as how kind, sincere, and trustworthy they are. Needless to say, nearly every woman I interviewed had experienced some form of this. One woman later found that her boyfriend had lied to her about virtually every aspect of his life—his age, his family, his previous jobs. The only thing he didn't lie about was his current job, and that was only because they worked together.

What makes deception an even bigger problem is that it turns out that, while seemingly all of us are reasonably adept at lying, we are terrible at telling when other people are lying to us. According to research, people can only distinguish truth from lies 54 percent of the time, which is not much better than random guessing. We're even worse at picking out lies, which we only manage to achieve 47 percent of the time. Sometimes even the person who is lying isn't aware that he or she is doing so, which makes detecting the lie nearly impossible.

Men are so quick to lie in order to have sex that evolutionary psychologist Glenn Geher advises women that if they can't judge a man's intention with at least 90 percent accuracy, they are better off being skeptical all the time. Women should also be more careful prior to entering a relationship. Once they are in a relationship, studies show that they tend to shut off their skepticism and become more vulnerable to deception. If you want to take a more active approach, you can try to train yourself to become better at figuring out when someone is lying, in which case you could turn to Paul Ekman, an expert on facial expressions. He has devoted a substantial part of his professional life to figuring out how to "read" deception in the face of other people and has found that our faces are constantly leaking information about what we are feeling. For example, if your boss makes an annoying request, you might cover up your feeling with a polite smile and a nod of assent, but there was likely a split second (less than a fifth of a second to be more precise) when your face sent a very different message, albeit too fleeting for your boss or even you to notice. Ekman calls these brief moments microexpressions, and with training, you can become better at noticing these facial "leaks."

Deception, genetic warfare, measures, and countermeasures—we are a long way from the romantic story line. Although evolutionary psychology offers a great deal of insight into human mating and dating, it is not a pretty picture. Luckily, that is not the end of the story.

WEIGHT SYMMETRY COMMITMENT MONOGAMY PENIS SIZE SMILES LIES INTERNET DA
NSCIOUS ROMANCE DESIRE MASTU...ATIONS CHEAP SPERM PRECIOUS EGG
SSFUL WOMEN YOUNGER MEN DEM...NG POOL MARRIAGE MARKET GIRL PC
TATUS MALE SELF-DECEPTION SEXUAL...BIG BALLS WAIST-TO-HIP RATIO SYMME

2 ½

The Dating Animal, Part II

How Dating Is What Makes Us Human or Darwin Reconsidered

BEFORE WE BECOME TOO DISHEARTENED ABOUT THE level of deception between men and women, we need to consider the role of deception in the development of the human mind. The old saying is that to err is human, but a more accurate statement might be to lie is human because it appears that social manipulation is at the core of how we became who we are. According to one study, people lie in about 25 percent of their regular daily interactions, which means that even the simplest of human exchanges often involve deception. Take, for example, the smile. Ekman is probably the leading expert in the world at decoding what our faces are actually expressing. What he has found about our smiles is nothing to smile at. He has uncovered nineteen different kinds of smile. How many of those are genuine expressions of pleasure or happiness? One! That's right. We have nineteen different ways to smile, and only one of them is a truly sincere expression of how we feel.

THE MACHIAVELLIAN MIND

Distressing though this is, our social skills (a much nicer expression than deception) are quite possibly the key to understanding how the human brain evolved. One of the leading theories for why human beings developed large brains is called the social brain hypothesis, also known rather chillingly as the Machiavellian intelligence theory. The idea is that the size of our social groups has played the essential role in pushing humans to develop larger brains. Many primates, such as chimpanzees, live in reasonably large troops, usually between twenty to fifty members. But no animal is more social and lives in larger groups than man. There are many advantages to larger groups, but there is one serious disadvantage: negotiating relationships with all the members of the group. Rewarding friends, seeking allies, and avoiding enemies all require more brainpower as the group gets larger. Researchers have found that the larger an animal's group size, the larger the percentage of the brain devoted to the neocortex (the outer layer of the brain, which accounts for most cognitive abilities). For most mammals, the neocortex makes up 30–40 percent of the brain. For highly social primates, such as chimpanzees, the percentage rises to 50 to 65 percent. For humans, the neocortex takes up a staggering 80 percent of the brain (and our brains are seven times larger than you would expect for a mammal of our size).

According to social brain theorists, the size of human groups also played a key role in the evolution of language. For other primates, the glue that keeps the group in relative harmony is grooming—that staple activity of animal behavior, for example, when one chimpanzee combs through the hair of another to untangle fur or remove nits. This is done not just for reasons of hygiene but also to reaffirm the social bond between the two. Primatologists have charted a linear relationship between the size of the group and the amount of time spent grooming. But grooming is time consuming, too time consuming for humans once their group size began to grow beyond fifty. Imagine trying to use grooming to hold together a large corporation. Nothing would ever get done. So, language came to serve as a kind of accelerated social grooming, allowing group members to maintain relationships on a much larger scale. For social brain theorists, language developed not primarily for informational tasks, such as where to find a wildebeest, but so that we could gossip about one another. Gossip served not as a distraction from the task at hand but as the main business, establishing and defining our relationships with other members of the group. Who shares meat, which person can't be trusted, who cheats on whom. Gossip became the means of handling our ever-expanding social networks. Lest you think we have evolved beyond that today, studies show that fully 60–70 percent of our conversations are devoted to social topics (i.e., gossip).

Of course, as Ekman's eighteen lying smiles already revealed, social life and gossip are firmly intertwined with deception. You see, a larger neocortex doesn't just predict the size of a species' social group. It also predicts how much that species uses duplicity and social manipulation. The proponents of the social brain theory are still wrestling with perhaps the central question it raises about our development: is our brain growth directed more toward enabling us to connect with one another or more toward allowing us to manipulate one another? Now you can see why this theory is also called Machiavellian.

If we take Darwin's idea of sexual selection seriously, though, we can narrow the driving force behind brain growth even further. We may, in fact, be able to pin it entirely on the need to find a mate. In other words, the central purpose behind our enormous brains may be to help us negotiate the unruly world of dating. Evolutionary psychologist Geoffrey Miller, a leading proponent of this theory, has even gone so far as to call the human mind a "protean courtship device."

The reason mating is a plausible force behind our brain growth is because of something known as runaway sexual selection, which occurs when both the trait and the preference for the trait are heritable. In this case, if the main social difficulty that we face as a species is securing a mate, and if the most essential trait to accomplish that is our intelligence, and if intelligence is heritable, then sexual selection will lead to greater intelligence. And if the *preference* for intelligence is also heritable, then sexual selection will boost human intelligence even more dramatically (this is where it becomes runaway). And what really supercharges runaway sexual selection in our species is that women are not the only ones looking for intelligence. Men also tend to want intelligence in their mates, although not quite as avidly as women. With both sides choosing for intelligence, you can see why "runaway" is a fairly apt description. I guess you could call this the Don Juan theory of human development.

Once you look at things through the lens of sexual selection, there is almost no aspect of human culture that remains untouched by it. Geoffrey Miller argues that most of our cultural behavior is largely instinctual and derived from sexual selection — not that we're conscious of it. This isn't a crude and straightforward expression of our sex drive or a case of Freudian sublimation; rather, sexual selection has hijacked qualities that were quite likely already being chosen through natural selection. To bolster his claim, Miller looked at when artists in different fields were most productive, and what he found was that male artists tend to peak around the age of thirty, which is strangely youthful if you think about the importance of artists maturing and developing, but an age that makes perfect sense if you think of artistic production as a means of attracting sexual partners. He also found that men produce vastly more than women. Of course, there is a cultural element to this, but Miller suggests that there is also a sexual element—that men are under more pressure to attract women (remember—cheap sperm, precious eggs). So, sexual selection taken to its logical extreme can explain virtually everything in human development from Bach to skyscrapers, because, at the end of the day, our intelligence has developed largely thanks to the pressures of finding a mate.

THE SEXY—OR AT LEAST SEXED—BRAIN

Even as both men and women have developed an extraordinarily large and complex neocortex, though, their brains have not grown in precisely the same way, which is exactly what we should expect given that each sex faces different evolutionary challenges. Before I delve into those differences, though, I want to make one thing absolutely clear: these remarks should not be taken as confirmation of sexual stereotypes. They are based on averages. On average, men may have a greater capacity for math, and women may have a better facility with language. But that does not mean that women can't be brilliant mathematicians or that men can't be excellent writers. Our sexual prejudices are so ingrained that the first part of that statement is essential, while no one needs to be reminded about the second part.

These sexual differences are not simply the result of cultural conditioning. They exist in the physical structure of the brain itself and are the result of a surge of testosterone released in male babies during fetal development. For example, women have roughly 11 percent more neurons in the part of the brain that handles language and hearing. Also, the hippocampus, which is the principal location of emotion and memory formation, is larger in women than men (perhaps finally providing an answer to many women's frustrated sense that men never remember anything). And the brain center for observing emotion in others is more developed in women than men. Men's brains tend to have larger areas devoted to action and aggression, and male brains devote more than two and half times the space than women's to sex, although scientists have not yet determined how large a portion is devoted to sports. Because of these differences, women on average tend to be better with language, and men tend to be better at math and map reading.

These differences are so fundamental that, according to one study, the way men and women find their way through the world is different. When you present men with a maze, they tend to use geometric reasoning to move through it. Women, on the other hand, use landmarks. Both groups struggle when you force them to use the other sex's method. And it is quite possible that even this is related to finding a mate because, in a statement so obvious I almost blush to write it, first you have to literally *find* a mate. Men's greater spatial skills when it comes to things like map reading likely aided them in their search. Women, as the precious egg holders, could sit around and wait for suitors to show themselves, much like Amanda Wingfield with her eighteen gentlemen callers in *The Glass Menagerie*. For evidence of this in the animal world, you only need look at the humble vole. We are interested in two particular species, the pine vole and the meadow vole. Pine voles are monogamous. The males and the females have similar brains, and each sex does about the same when required to run through a maze. The meadow vole, however, is polygamous, and males have to cover much greater distances than the females because they have to visit the different burrows of their various female partners. Not only does a male meadow vole have a bigger hippocampus than the female, he also is much better at finding his way through a maze. This may finally explain men's unwillingness to ask for help when lost. Before the age of GPS, the ability to find one's way was probably one of the tests of a man's genetic fitness.

Needless to say, there are some fairly obvious differences when it comes to sex and the brain. When researchers scanned the brains of people watching a neutral conversation between a man and a woman, the male brains immediately showed activity in the sexual areas, while the women's brains did not. As Louann

Brizendine aptly put it in her fascinating book *The Female Brain*, men have an eight-lane superhighway in their brains when it comes to sex, while women have an eight-lane superhighway when it comes to emotion. But it's not just sex. It appears that men and women also tend to fall in love differently. For men in love, the visual areas of the brain are the most active, while for women a number of different areas are involved.

This confirms what we have already found about human behavior, but what is fascinating is how the female brain has developed in ways that help women counter the ferocious sex drives of men. This is where her greater facility with language and emotion come into play. As we have seen, men are perfectly willing to lie about themselves or about their commitment in order to have sex, so women have to be good at spotting that deception. And a number of studies have found that women *are* better at reading the facial expression and emotional nuances of an encounter. For example, in one study, men were able to pick up signs of sadness in a female face only 40 percent of the time, while women succeeded 90 percent of the time. Women's brains are also designed to remember the emotional details of an encounter. So, even on the level of brain development, men and women appear to be locked in an evolutionary struggle, what Geoffrey Miller has called "a never-ending arms race of romantic skepticism and excess." And women continually hone their abilities as well. As I discussed in the last chapter, researchers have found that women often have detailed talks decoding encounters with the opposite sex or analyzing the character of a man, while men tend not to talk about those things very much.

This will hardly come as a shock—women, after all, flock to *Sex and the City*, while men tune in to *Entourage*.

One controversial theory is that autism might be the result of an overly masculinized brain. I don't want to make light of a serious condition, but given the vast differences on average between men and women when it comes to dealing with the intricacies of human relationships, such as intuiting the emotions of another, I think many women might find it useful when dating and even in long-term relationships to think of most men as slightly autistic compared to women.

THE IMPORTANCE OF WAIST-TO-HIP RATIOS AND OTHER ODD METRICS OF ATTRACTION

Okay, so we have these big brains, but are they hardwired to look for certain things? The romantic story line says no, claiming that we are all unique and that love itself is as varied as a snowflake. In this view, beauty is in the eye of the beholder. Love is blind. Yadda yadda yadda. But the scientific answer to this question is a resounding yes. Although science cannot explain the idiosyncratic reasons why you may prefer a partner who likes piña coladas, it can do a better job with general explanations of why you are attracted to someone than you can yourself.

First of all, let's ditch the idea that beauty is subjective. It's not. Studies have shown that even babies prefer attractive faces, so these preferences seem to be virtually hardwired into us—so much so that when hooked up to electrodes, people looking at beautiful female faces generated an extra electrical charge. And surveys show that there is strong agreement about whom people find attractive. Interestingly, composite pictures melding numerous faces always outscore individual faces in attractiveness and become more attractive the more faces you include, for the simple reasons that a more symmetrical face is the result. As we've already seen with the female orgasm, we're big fans—albeit unwittingly—of symmetricality. Understanding why reveals the excellent evolutionary reasons for the way our desires have been shaped. In this case, being symmetrical is an excellent proxy for our general health. And how symmetrical you are is an excellent sign not just of how healthy you are *now* but also how healthy you have always been, since asymmetries tend to occur because of disease or illness during our fetal and childhood development. Hair is another good indicator, which helps explain the vast array of products directed at creating better-looking hair. Long, lustrous hair signals an equally long and robust good health. Skin acts as a similar signpost of health.

According to one theory, evolution has even added a wrinkle so that people with excellent genes can show off their fitness by displaying what evolutionary biologist Amotz Zahavi dubbed a "high cost signal." Think back to Darwin and his original formulation of the survival of the fittest. When it comes to the utilitarian selection of certain qualities essential for the survival of a species—a gazelle's speed or a bear's claws—efficiency rules. When it comes to sexual selection, though, signaling to the opposite sex can involve a good bit of waste. Take, for example, the male peacock's tail. It's enormous, using a tremendous amount

of the bird's resources and making him more vulnerable to predators. But what it also does is signal to the female that he is so
healthy, he doesn't need to worry about hoarding his resources.
In this way, the male peacock is able to distinguish himself from
his moderately healthy peers. The high-cost signal can take all
sorts of forms—think of the man who buys an expensive sports
car as a signal that he has resources to burn. But we humans, like
other animals, already have all sorts of high-cost "signals" built
into us—as well as an unconscious desire to look for them in the
opposite sex.

Think of the typical ideal for a man's face—a large, square,
"manly" jaw and chin. This ideal is so dominant that it is almost
a visual cliché in our culture, and you would be hard-pressed
to find a Hollywood leading man who doesn't have that look.
It turns out that women's preference for that particular face is
not merely some arbitrary aesthetic whim. You need a lot of testosterone during puberty to produce a face like that. The problem is that testosterone also suppresses the immune system and
makes a young man more vulnerable to disease, so the ability to
have such a face serves as a high-cost signal of genetic fitness.
Only extremely fit individuals can afford that face and remain
disease free.

Women have their own bodily signals. For instance, there is
a very good reason men prefer full lips and why someone like
Angelina Jolie is almost freakishly genetically fit. Although
not a high-cost signal, those full lips require a woman to be
hyperfeminine—at least when it comes to sex hormones. During
puberty, the woman must experience both a surge of estrogen
and a low level of testosterone. This also will give her a shorter,

lower face, which will further feminize her look. And it turns out that there may be perfectly good evolutionary reasons why gentlemen prefer blondes. Blond hair is one of those traits that changes dramatically with age. Men who prefer blondes are likely unconsciously choosing them because their hair signals health and fecundity. One theory for why blond hair evolved in northern Europe is that the cold weather kept people covered in clothes so that women had to develop a way to advertise their youth that could be seen. Hence, blond hair.

One of the best indicators of female genetic fitness is a rather bizarre ratio that most people have never heard of, let alone consciously considered. Waist-to-hip ratio. That's right—not breast size or any of the other more obvious markers of beauty, but waist-to-hip ratio, which has an enormous influence on whether or not men find a woman attractive (the comparable male ratio is waist-to-shoulder). It turns out that the ideal ratio is 0.7 or, in layman's terms, an hourglass figure. In one ingenious study, a researcher examined centerfolds from *Playboy* and beauty contest winners from the past several decades. While the women did get thinner on average during that period, their waist-to-hip ratio held steady at 0.7. Women may worry about being fat, but it turns out that it's not how fat you are but how that fat is distributed. For example, one study found that heavy women with a low waist-to-hip ratio were preferred to thin women with a high ratio. Again, there is a very good reason for men's preference. That waist-to-hip ratio is an excellent indicator not just of good health (many diseases have been linked to the ratios in which fat is distributed) but also of high fertility. A study of Polish women revealed that women with low waist-to-hip ratios also had high fecundity as measured by their reproductive hormones. And scientists have recently discovered yet another advantage. Fat in a woman's hips and thighs is particularly good fat because there is a higher concentration of omega-3 fatty acids (which are important for brain development). A recent study has shown that children of these curvy mothers have better cognitive abilities than children of the less curvy, and the bigger the difference between the waist and the hips, the better the children did.

Because of our built-in preference for attractive people, those who are genetically blessed enjoy all sorts of additional societal advantages beyond simply finding a mate. For instance, one study revealed the power of attractiveness to create personal space. Researchers placed a beautiful woman on a busy street corner and found that people will give her more room than an unattractive woman. And growing up with good looks imbues the person with an inherent self-confidence. In one study, people were made to wait while a psychiatrist conducted a phone conversation. The real purpose of the study was to see how long people would wait before they interrupted. Attractive people waited on average three minutes and twenty seconds. Unattractive people waited nine minutes. And here's the kicker: when both groups were asked to rate their assertiveness, they gave themselves equal marks! That shows how ingrained these tendencies become and how they are hidden not just from the individuals but from society in general. It turns out that a great deal of what we assume about someone's personality might largely be the result of something like attractiveness. Female attractiveness even appears to make men behave stupidly. Well, okay, maybe that's a little harsh, but one study did find that if you show men pictures of beautiful women, the men are more likely to stop thinking about the long-term consequences of their actions. And if they are turned on, watch out. According to another study, men in a state of arousal are more likely to respond positively to almost any suggestion from the merely kinky (do you find women's shoes erotic?) to the downright disturbing (would you slip a woman a drug to increase the chance that she would have sex with you?).

Your attractiveness also has an effect on the sex of your children. Attractive parents have an increased chance of having a daughter (56 percent, rather than 48 percent). Evolutionary psychologists have speculated that the increase is an evolutionary attempt to maximize the advantages of looks, since those qualities are far more valued in women than men, although they have no idea what the biological mechanism is that causes attractive parents to have more female babies.

WHY YOUNG WOMEN END UP WITH OLD MEN AND NOT VICE VERSA

Up to this point, we have not discussed human personality traits, but there is a great deal of evidence that evolution has shaped these as well. Humor, kindness, empathy—all of them help attract a mate, and all have likely developed at least in part due to sexual selection. The No. 1 task that we have evolved to perform (besides simply staying alive) is to attract a mate and reproduce. Because of this, no aspect of our humanity can be separated from the process of sexual selection. So, it's not just our intelligence that is a product of evolution. Virtually every aspect of our personality is. The question is, what personal qualities *do* men and women look for in one another? We'll explore this topic more closely in chapter 5, but there is an incredibly simple answer to the question.

If you want to boil all this down to its most essential level, men look for youth and beauty in their partners, and women want wealth and status. In one study of personal ads, women mentioned financial success in their ads eleven times more than men did, and men mentioned attractiveness three times more often than women did. To illustrate how strikingly obvious this is, I want you to call to mind one of the many times you have seen a young, attractive woman with a very old but very successful man. For instance, consider 1993 Playmate of the Year Anna Nicole Smith, who was twenty-six when she married eighty-nine-year-old oil billionaire J. Howard Marshall. Not very hard to think of older men–younger women couplings, is it? Now, try to remember the last time you saw the opposite: a young, attractive man with a very old and very successful woman. It's not so easy to think of examples of that.

In a completely unsurprising confirmation of this observation, studies show that beautiful women end up with rich men far more often than beautiful men end up with rich women. Seeing an older man with a younger woman is commonplace and merely takes to a logical extreme a man's desire for a young partner and a woman's desire for a financially successful man, but an older woman with a younger man violates those norms. There is no cultural reason why this should be the case. Our shock can be traced directly to how evolution has shaped us.

Looks are so important to men that, according to one study, the physical attractiveness of a wife is a better indicator of a man's occupational status than any of her other qualities: better than her intelligence, her socioeconomic status, or her education. Another study has shown that the more attractive an adolescent girl is, the more likely she will marry up (the more sexually active an adolescent girl is, the less likely she will marry up). All of this is not an indication of American shallowness. David Buss has researched thirty-seven cultures around the globe and has found that these preferences show up in every single one of them. In fact, non-Western cultures tend to place an even greater value on female attractiveness because it is a valuable indication of physical health in an environment rife with parasites and other health problems.

Before women judge men too harshly, though, they should recognize that men's obsession with youthfulness is likely the result of monogamy. Because men are choosing a lifelong partner, there is added pressure to choose someone young who will be fertile for many years. In more promiscuous species, biologists have found that the males exhibit no bias for younger partners. In addition, women have their own set of preferences, which they cling to just as tenaciously. For example, height. Women are nuts about it. Although that seems shallow, especially when the guy can just buy lifts, height is an excellent evolutionary indicator of health. In fact, demographers use height as one measure to judge national health and prosperity. Unfortunately, the national news on this front is not good. The United States once had the tallest and healthiest citizens in the world but now ranks near the bottom of industrialized nations. While other nations have been tacking nearly an inch per decade onto their average (due to things like better access to health care and a more equitable division of wealth), Americans haven't done so since the 1970s so that northern Europeans now tower an average of three inches over us.

None of this means that men and women don't value many of the same things. Both sexes, for example, place importance on dependability and stability. But in far more cases than the casual observer may suppose, the sexes are driven by fundamentally different urges.

All of this contains one important lesson for men and women. Hearing women complain about how men prefer younger women or men complain about how women only care about money is probably as old as civilization. Evolution has planted those desires so deeply into us that it's a waste of energy to fight them. The simple truth is that you are not going to change such fundamental drives, and any change that does occur will happen slowly over many generations. You may wish for men and women to be different, but if you want to succeed in the Darwinian world of dating, you must deal with them as they are.

A Brief Intermission to Consider the Question of Monogamy

BEFORE WE GO ANY FURTHER, WE SHOULD EXPLORE PER-haps the most basic question about the relationship between a man and a woman in today's society: just how suited are we for monogamy?

SLIGHTLY POLYGAMOUS MAN

You don't need the last chapter to realize that men—and women—cheat in such astonishing numbers that it makes one wonder how any couple manages the feat of staying together. The truth is that monogamy is a highly unusual arrangement in both the animal kingdom and the human world. Ninety percent of animal species are polygamous. For mammals, the trend is even more pronounced—97 percent are polygamous. A look back through time reveals that monogamy is also extremely rare in human societies. In one study of past and present societies for which anthropologists were able to collect data, they found that 980 out of the 1,154 societies allowed men to have more than one wife. That's almost 85 percent! Of course, that statistic hides the fact that even in polygamous societies, monogamy is the norm. Multiple wives are expensive, and usually only 5 to 10 percent of the men can afford more than one wife, so most of the men are (and were) monogamous whether they wanted to be or not. And polygamy is not just men with multiple wives (known more precisely as polygyny). You can also find a few examples of societies where women have more than one husband (polyandry). This tends to occur in extremely difficult conditions when several men, usually brothers, are needed to produce enough food to raise one child, such as certain societies in Nepal.

But you don't have to rely on anthropological evidence to see our proclivity for polygamy. Our polygamous past is literally written onto our bodies. To answer the question of just how monogamous we are, we need to make another foray into the world of biology. One fairly good indicator of the extent of polygamy in a species is the size disparity between males and females—the more polygamous a species, the more males must fight to obtain harems. In the battle for dominance, size is usually the decisive factor, with the larger males monopolizing the females. Their size advantage is then passed along to their offspring so that the males continue to grow larger over time (in biological terms, women's bodies shouldn't be considered smaller versions of men's bodies; rather, women are the norm, and men's bodies should be considered larger versions of women's bodies). When a species is monogamous, males and females will be similar in size. For gibbons, a monogamous ape species, the males and females are virtually equal in size. For gorillas, whose successful males typically have harems of three to six females, the males are nearly twice the size of females. You can see this in an even more extreme form with the southern elephant seal. On average, the harem size for a male elephant seal is forty-eight females, so the male is enormous compared to the female—fully three tons compared to seven hundred pounds.

How about human beings? Men are roughly 10 percent taller and 20 percent heavier than women, which indicates mild polygamy. Applying a formula developed by biologists, we can estimate that male body size indicates harems of two to three women. But there is some good news. We appear to be evolving in a more monogamous direction. A few hundred thousand years ago, men used to be one and half times the size of females, so our current 20 percent difference represents a distinct decrease. If we give it another couple of hundred thousand years, we may find that men and women match each other exactly and live in perfect monogamous bliss. Of course, this measurement may no longer be as relevant as it once was. Men don't go around these days competing for women using feats of strength. The competition tends to be mental, rather than physical, which may also account for the shrinking size differential.

. . . AND SLIGHTLY PROMISCUOUS WOMAN

Before women start bemoaning men's lackluster commitment to monogamy, they should realize that there are also indicators that women are quite likely to stray from monogamy as well. In this instance, the key measurement is testicle size because testicle size and sperm production vary directly in relation to female promiscuity. The reason for this is quite simple—sperm competition. If a female has sex with multiple partners during ovulation, the more sperm a male can ejaculate increases his chances of being the father. Chimpanzees live in large social groups where there is a high degree of promiscuity among the troop—so much so that male chimps can rarely, if ever, be sure of the paternity of a baby chimp. Not surprisingly, chimps have enormous testicles. Gorillas, on the other hand, live in much different circumstances. A male is the only one to mate with his harem as long as he remains unchallenged. Consequently, a gorilla's testicles are quite small. The comparison between the two species is nothing short of astonishing. Despite being only a quarter the size of gorillas, chimpanzees have testicles that are roughly four times larger. Adjusted for body weight, the disparity is even greater. Biologists have found a similar link between testicle size and mating systems of birds—the largest testicles were found in species where several males fertilize one female.

So just where do human beings fall on this scale? Somewhere in the middle, although closer to the big ball end of the spectrum. Men's testes weigh in at an average of two and a half ounces. Our testicles are roughly the size of a gorilla's, even though a gorilla weighs roughly 450 pounds, and the average man weighs only 175 pounds. A chimpanzee's testicles are almost twice as large as our own, even though a male chimpanzee weighs on average one hundred pounds. To give a rough approximation based on body size, male gorillas' testicles are only .02 percent of their body weight.

Human males are .08 percent, and chimps' testicles are a whopping .03 percent. Although we fall far short of our chimpanzee cousins, the size of our testes is a clear indication that throughout our history women have typically had more than one simultaneous sexual partner and that sperm competition was a regular part of our past. Of course, the king of balls is not Stephen Colbert but the right whale. The females mate with multiple males, so the males have developed big balls. I'm talking really big balls—each testicle weighs roughly a quarter of a ton.

Again, though, there is some evidence that humans are evolving in a more monogamous direction. Given the size of a man's testicles, the amount of sperm that he produces is on the lower end of the scale compared to other mammals, which means that our ancestors' testicles were probably producing a lot more sperm than we are today. This is likely a sign of decreasing sexual competition and stronger pair-bonds. Men also store fewer sperm than other animals, and fully 25 percent of a man's sperm is defective on average compared to only 5 percent for chimps. When it comes to multiple ejaculations, men are the ninety-eight-pound weaklings of the animal kingdom. A male chimpanzee can ejaculate five times in five hours and still have more than half his sperm stored in his testicles. The mighty and aptly named ram can ejaculate thirty to forty times a day, and each ejaculation contains more than eight times the amount of sperm that the average man produces in one ejaculation (and that's leaving aside the fact that the man will need a nap before he even thinks about round two, let alone round forty).

On a side note, despite their anxieties, men can be quite proud of how their penises stack up against the primate competition. The average erect penis is a little under six inches with a circumference slightly under five inches (although most studies of male penis size are exaggerated because they rely on self-reported measurements). By comparison, the chimp has an erect penis of three inches. The orangutan measures a measly one and a half inches. And the mighty gorilla weighs in with a tiny one-and-a-quarter-inch penis (if you go outside the primate world, the lowly slug turns out to be the genital giant of our planet—at least in relation to body size—having a penis that is several times longer than its actual body!). Biologists are still arguing about why men have such large penises. It seems that the most likely answer has nothing to do with procreation but is about what is called a "threat display." In other words, the penis probably once functioned much as a stag's antlers do—as a visible display of masculinity (at least until pants became widespread).

But to return to the original question, why has our society chosen monogamy when there are so many signs of our tendency toward polygamy? The answer is the same as that discussed in the last chapter: the survival of children. Monogamy becomes more prevalent in an environment where food is scarce, and predators are common. By increasing the bonds between husband and wife, monogamy also increases the certainty of the paternity of the children, which in turn increases the willingness of the father to play a larger role in providing for his family.

MONOGAMY'S WINNERS AND LOSERS

Most women reading this are probably thinking what a good thing it is that polygamy was ditched in favor of monogamy. And there are probably a few men reading this who are feeling nostalgic for a time when men could be men and have as many wives as they could support. But the irony is that monogamy tends to benefit most men and hurt most women. One economist has even called anti-polygamy laws a kind of male cartel undermining women's bargaining ability. On the other hand, polygamy benefits most women and hurts most men. I realize most women would not consider it a dating triumph to be some man's second wife. When I say "benefit," what I mean is how valuable a mate one can attract. You see, it's all a question of numbers. With polygamy, low-status men are the worst off. They have to struggle to secure any sort of mate. One of the social problems of polygamous societies is the murderous competition that they create among low-status men (incidentally, they also help explain the appeal of suicide bombing to young Muslim men of low status, since part of their promised reward is a harem of seventy-two virgins in the afterlife). Our founding myths are a testament to the struggle to secure the best females. The epic conflict in Homer's *Iliad* is over the possession of a single woman.

For women, though, polygamy offers them tremendous opportunities to upgrade their spouses. An average-looking woman can settle for an average husband, or she can choose to be the second wife of a high-status man. Women might initially scoff at this idea, but if you presented them with a choice between being Brad Pitt's second wife or Homer Simpson's first wife, I think we know which one most of them would choose.

In a monogamous society, though, the competition among women is vastly increased, while the competition among men is significantly lessened. And if the population in a monogamous society shifts slightly so that there are more women than men, the competition between females can become as fierce as any in the animal kingdom. I'm not suggesting that women agitate for a repeal of bigamy laws, but it helps to understand how the rules and values of our society can have unrealized consequences for the competition to secure a mate.

Our sometimes wobbly commitment to monogamy should not be surprising. Notice the way that major institutions—the church and the state to name the big ones—have been mobilized to strengthen the bonds of matrimony. Even so, there are many ways to make end runs around the system. Many people engage in a kind of serial monogamy today, dating or even marrying for a few years and then moving on to the next partner. In effect, this serves as a kind of slow-motion polygamy. Think of the rich and successful men who repeatedly divorce in order to marry younger women. And there are other loopholes, such as adultery.

So, it is important to recognize that monogamy is rife with difficulties for human beings. As one book aptly titled *The Myth of Monogamy* suggests, monogamy is not ordained by natural law but is instead a fragile compromise in the ongoing battle between men and women. No less an authority than Margaret Mead called monogamy the hardest of all human marital arrangements.

3

The Dating Culture

What I Learned About Dating from Thorstein Veblen

A H, BUT WE ARE NOT SIMPLY THE SUM OF OUR EVOLU-tionary urges, our concealed ovulations and big balls and deceptive smiles. We are shaped by our rich and complicated cultures. The good news is that cultural evolution occurs much more quickly than genetic evolution, so there is every possibility that our culture could change in a variety of ways that make both dating and relationships easier in the future. In contrast to other species, humans have shown enormous flexibility in their mating arrangements throughout the course of history, which reveals the important and variable role of culture in our lives. In our current case, though, our culture is not doing a lot of favors for people interested in a happy, long-term relationship. In fact, there are very compelling cultural reasons why dating and relationships have become a vexing problem for many of us.

I must warn you that this chapter is somewhat eclectic. It discusses everything from consumerism to demographics. In my to ziplock bags. Well, it turns out that our abundance of choices may not be such a good thing. In fact, it may be a very bad thing. But, first, let's explore the conundrum of too many jams, which will shed some light on one aspect of our current dating woes, strange as that may sound.

A group of researchers set up a sample table of high-quality jams in a gourmet food store to find out what happens when you present people with choice. Any customer who sampled a jam was given a dollar-off coupon if they bought a jar. Free taste of jam, one dollar off, what could be better? But those clever researchers introduced one variable—the amount of choice on offer. On one day, the researchers set up the table with six varieties of jam for tasting. On another day, they offered twenty-four different jams. The same twenty-four were always available for purchase, regardless of the day, but consumers either had six to sample or a bewildering twenty-four. As you might expect, the vast array of twenty-four samples attracted more customers, although the rest of the tale does not turn out quite how one would imagine. Whether six samples or twenty-four are on offer, people taste about the same number on average. But the shocking part of the study came when the researchers tallied up how many people bought jam. When only six samples were offered, 30 percent of the samplers ended up purchasing a jar. When customer were offered twenty-four samples, though, a paltry 3 percent bought a jar. In other words, in the face of virtually endless choice, consumers locked up. They froze. They failed to make it over the most basic hurdle essential to a consumer society— they didn't buy anything! Perhaps you think that jams offer some element of complexity that undid the tasters. Some conundrum involving the subtle implications of pectins, say. So, the researchers ran a similar test in the controlled environment of a laboratory with chocolates, and they came up with strikingly similar results.

What's going on here? The researchers give a number of explanations, but let's focus on the big picture. Our entire economy is predicated on the idea that more choice is always better, but what these studies show is that more choice is sometimes worse. Give people enough choice, and it makes it difficult for them to make any decision at all. As Barry Schwartz has written in his excellent book on the subject, *The Paradox of Choice*, "At this point, choice no longer liberates, but debilitates. It might even be said to tyrannize."

It doesn't even take that much choice. You can create difficulties for people with only three alternatives when two of the choices are roughly similar. What if I offered you a dollar and a half for filling out a survey or a pen worth two dollars? When researchers offered students precisely this choice, roughly 75 percent of the participants chose the pen. Then the researchers ran the study again—only this time, participants were offered three choices, one dollar fifty, a nice two-dollar pen, or two less-expensive pens worth two dollars. Any rational analysis of the choice based on the previous study would suggest that at least as high a percentage of students would choose either the two-dollar pen or the two pens. In fact, we might even predict that the number would go up because some students may not like nice pens and would prefer the inexpensive ones. But that isn't what happened. Instead of sticking with the pens, a majority of students opted for the money. The question is, why? The researchers argue that it was too difficult for most students to choose between the two kinds of pen, so they simply decided to forego that decision and choose the money.

Perhaps choosing a pen is too insubstantial to prove anything definitive about decision making. But what if I told you that professionals, trained for years to make certain kinds of decisions, were flummoxed in exactly the same way as the students? It's true. A group of doctors had the same difficulty choosing among three alternative medical treatments when two of them were similar and changed their decision in exactly the same "irrational" way.

So what does all this have to do with love? Nothing if you believe in the romantic story line—and everything if you want to look at love through the lens of science. Imagine that you are trying to choose among three potential boyfriends. Two are similar. Let's say they are both young associates at a law firm who like to play golf on the weekends. The third is a musician who keeps odd hours and promises to write a song about you. In the end, you choose the musician. If you believe the romantic story line, your choice reflected an innate sense that the musician was the right partner for you. If you believe the science, there is a very good chance that you chose the musician to avoid the complexity of choosing between similar alternatives.

This is exactly what I have found in my interviews with men and women. When most of them tried to choose among several people at the same time, they had enormous difficulty. As one of them said to me, "No one is perfect, so you are left trying to compare very different traits." Not only did these people feel more uncertainty about their choices, they had more difficulty even deciding on what grounds they should choose. A couple of them admitted to being so immobilized that they never made any choice and simply waited for some of the people to fall away until they were left with only one option.

The reason that choice is increasingly becoming not just a consumer problem but a dating problem is that we value quantity as the means of achieving quality, even when it comes to trying to meet someone. You only have to look at the explosion of Internet dating to see how the consumer model of expanding choice is shaping our approach to relationships. Fill out a personality profile, click on a few criteria, and you are suddenly presented with hundreds, if not thousands, of possibilities. According to a recent Pew study of online dating, people think that is a good thing, and they use Internet sites because they believe that having lots of choices will lead to a better match. But studies have shown that this increased choice is having exactly the effect that the consumer research would suggest. In one study of online dating, fewer than 1 percent of possible candidates are chosen. One woman admitted to me that, in an effort to cut down on her choices, she developed absurd physical criteria. Another confessed to endless scanning of profiles and said, "With ten thousand page views to go, you feel like you can't afford not to be choosy." A man I interviewed dubbed his Internet dating compulsion the "curse of the composite." Over time, he has developed a vision of his ideal woman based on the various qualities that he likes—only now he has created a composite standard that is impossible to meet. He is thinking of taking a break from Internet dating because he believes it is eroding his ability to commit to a single woman.

And that's leaving aside the whole issue of deception and Internet dating. If lying is a problem for regular dating, it's an epidemic for Internet dating. Various studies estimate that between one-fifth and one-third of all online daters are married, and that is just the tip of the iceberg. Stories abound of photos that are twenty years out of date or forty pounds lighter. Wall Street bankers who turn out to be Wall Street baristas. One woman has had so many outlandishly terrible experiences using Yahoo Personal Ads that she has rechristened the site "Yahoo Psychos" with even more colorful nicknames for the men themselves. The situation is so bad that some dating sites base their appeal on weeding out the duplicitous and undesirable. The dating site True.com even runs criminal checks on its members—although, as far as I know, pretending to be much younger, better looking, and successful than you actually are is not a criminal offense, even though it may feel that way to the other person when he or she finally meets the prevaricator in person.

BUYER'S REMORSE

It's not just that having too many choices makes choosing more difficult. Having too many choices actually breeds both bad choices and dissatisfaction with the choices that you do make. Let's look first at how difficult it is for most of us to make good choices. When presented with an array of possibilities, we do what any good consumer has been trained to do. We comparison shop (something that dating on the Internet has made almost compulsory), but it turns out that we are often misled by the comparisons. In one study, volunteers were asked how much they would enjoy eating potato chips. One group was asked this while sitting at a table with a bag of potato chips next to a choco-late bar, while another group was faced with a can of sardines next to the potato chips. As astute students of human nature, you can probably guess what happened next. Volunteers who were looking at the can of sardines predicted that they would enjoy eating the potato chips much more than those looking at the chocolate bar. Even though they weren't choosing between two alternatives, they couldn't stop themselves from comparing them. Of course, when the two groups ate the potato chips, the comparison became irrelevant, and both groups enjoyed the chips equally. But comparison had led them astray.

The problem is that in our need to distinguish between differ-ent things, we often seize upon some quality that may not have much to do with our ultimate satisfaction—or may not even ex-ist. In another study, shoppers were presented with four pairs of identical panty hose and asked to choose the highest-quality pair. People had no difficulty choosing one identical pair over another (almost no one who participated noticed that they were identi-cal). The biggest influence on their choice? Where the panty hose were placed—40 percent of people preferred the panty hose on the far right.

But the problems with too much choice don't end once a decision has been made. Too much choice makes us more dis-satisfied *whatever we choose*. That's right. Even if it turns out later that we made the "best" choice, we still find ourselves more un-happy. Why? The problem is that comparing different things makes you aware of the trade-offs, how each choice involves giv-ing up something you might very well like. And we hate the idea that we have to give things up. The irony is that those people who work the hardest to make the right decision—the truly indefatigable bargain hunters out there—end up the most dissatisfied of all, according to surveys, even if they have objectively made the correct decision.

Once you consider these problems, it can make you rethink your entire relationship history because our romantic choices are subject to the same confusions that we find in any instance when people face numerous choices. Who among us has not at one time or another experienced this romantic version of buyer's remorse? No matter how excited we are, at some point in the future our feelings about the beloved will fade. The amazing part is not that this occurs time and time again, but that, according to studies ranging from consumer purchases to major life changes, we seem to be unable to remember that it occurs, so we experience the same cycle of excitement and disappointment each and every time. A little like Charlie Brown and the football.

CAN'T I JUST CHOOSE AGAIN?

Of course, our romantic mistakes can always be undone these days, which you would think is a good thing. But the very reversibility of our romantic commitments has only worsened our problem because that *also* undermines our satisfaction with our choices. To see this, you only need to look at a study of a group of college students in a photography class. The students made a print of their two best photographs. They were then told that they could choose one of the photos but that the other would be kept on file as an example of their work. Then, the teacher added a twist. One group was told that their choice was final. Whatever they chose, they could not change their minds later. The other group was told that they could switch photographs if they changed their minds. In a survey taken later, students who were allowed to change their mind liked their photos less than the other students. A similar study was done that allowed students the chance to return an art poster that they selected, and researchers found the same results—students who could reverse their decisions ended up liking their posters less. Why this paradoxical result? According to one researcher, the brain has a kind of built-in defense system that works to make us satisfied with choices that cannot be undone. Despite thinking that we would like the freedom to change our minds, it appears that we are happier with our choices if we think they can't be changed, which means we would be better off if we made romantic commitments more permanent and more difficult to break, rather than less.

Think this doesn't apply to relationships? Let's take a quick look at a popular relationship choice that comes with its own opt-out clause: cohabitation. As numerous studies have found, couples that live together are less likely to get married. But the effect of cohabitation doesn't stop there. Even if the couples do marry, they have an increased chance of divorce because it appears that living together weakens people's commitment to marriage. This is a rather startling statistic when you consider that more than half of serious couples live together as a kind of pre-marriage trial. And if you pair it with the consumer research, you come to a rather shocking conclusion: the ability to change our minds romantically (which doesn't stop at the altar anymore) is almost certainly hurting our relationships. I'm not arguing that people should stay in unhappy marriages, but I am saying that the ease with which we can leave a marriage is contributing to our unhappiness. It's no surprise that the rise of divorce has occurred at the same time that marriage—at least in rhetorical terms—has gradually been stripped of all of its practical roles until a choice of life partner has been reduced to one single criteria: personal fulfillment. This is the same criteria that dominates our consumer choices, so we tend to treat it like a consumer choice as well and endlessly scan the horizon wondering if someone better is going to come along.

Imagine a dating world where the opposite rules applied, where people were not given the freedom to opt into or out of a relationship, such as a culture that still practices arranged marriages. What researchers have found will seem pretty amazing to Westerners weaned on the romantic story line. According to a study by two Indian researchers, the levels of self-reported love in arranged marriages increased over time until they surpassed the level of self-reported love in marriages that were freely chosen. Incredible as it sounds, people with a very limited say in choosing their own spouses eventually became happier with their relationship than people with the freedom to choose anyone they wanted. Think of all the advantages that the unfettered couples have. They know each other's personalities and their tastes and whether or not there is any physical attraction, and so on. Despite all of that, the arranged marriages do better over the long haul. Why? I believe the secret has a lot to do with the discontent that is a by-product of a society predicated on choice. Cultures that use arranged marriages also frown on divorce, so a married couple knows that they are going to have to make things work. If the relationship sours, they face a lifetime of marital misery, and that offers a powerful incentive for making the best of things. To misquote JFK, it creates a mind-set where you ask not what your marriage can do for you but what you can do for your marriage. Western marriages place such a premium on personal fulfillment that the opposite mind-set prevails.

I'm not advocating a return to arranged marriages. I'm still a fan, albeit a critical one, of romantic love. But I do think that arranged marriages have a valuable lesson to teach all of us consumers. In Schwartz's terms, we need to learn to be "satisficers," rather than "maximizers." What does that mean? Maximizers are the tireless shoppers of the consumer world. They search out every option, try every product, and work very hard to get the best there is. Satisficers search only until they find something good enough, and then they stop looking. Living in a consumer society has a strong tendency to make us into maximizers. And while maximizers may find a better deal, studies show that they are less happy, less optimistic, and more depressed. In looking for love, the time has come for us to learn to be satisficers, not maximizers. That does not necessarily mean settling, but it does mean giving up on the idea of "the one." When you find someone you think will make you happy, you stop looking, even though there might be someone better out there. Don't feel that you have to sample every flavor, to chase every opportunity. As the students who sampled all those jams discovered, there is such a thing as too much jam—and too much choice. And there can also be too much dating. If you follow that path, you're likely to feel less satisfied, no matter whom you choose.

KEEPING UP WITH THE JONESES

Of course, any consideration of consumer society comes with its own neatly prepackaged moral problem, consumerism's evil henchman—envy. Call it what you will—keeping up with the Joneses, the rat race, status anxiety—the simple fact is that our culture generates a lot of envy and that envy has crept into our judgments about our relationships as well. I live in New York, which is an envy engine if ever there was one. The city not only has greater concentrations of wealth than ever before—it also has created a greater scope to display that wealth than ever before with everything from restaurants that cost one thousand dollars a person to apartments that cost tens of millions of dollars. Imagine Thorstein Veblen's theory of conspicuous consumption on steroids, and you have a pretty good idea of what I'm talking about.

Unfortunately, all of our struggles to get ahead have put a kink in our souls. Being rich is great, but it turns out that being richer than other people is what really gets our juices flowing. Most of us can accept the fact that in the big scheme of things we are not going to be the wealthiest person in the country or the state or even the city we live in, but we damn well want to make sure that we are the richest on the block. There are plenty of studies to back this up. For instance, a group of students were presented with a simple choice: would you rather live in a world where you made $50,000 a year, while other people made $25,000, or a world in which you made $100,000 while other

people made $200,000? The majority said that they would prefer
to live in the first world. In other words, what was most important
to the students was not their *absolute* wealth but their *relative*
wealth compared to other people. Researchers have asked similar questions about IQ and education. Time after time, a majority chose the option that improved their relative position. Not
only that, but we always assume the grass is greener. When we
compare ourselves to other people, studies show that we overestimate how great things are for our neighbors.

In many ways, we are mired once again in the problem of
comparison shopping but with a twist—more important than
finding the best car or the nicest house is finding one that is better than those of the people around you. And relationships do
not escape the pernicious effect of this desire. Just think of how
saturated our world is with advertisements filled with beautiful
people, and imagine the effect this has on the way we view our
romantic partners. In one study, groups of men were shown photographs of either highly attractive women or average women
and then asked to judge their commitment to their current romantic partner. Men who looked at the attractive women judged
their partner to be less attractive than the men who viewed the
average women. Worse, the men who viewed the attractive
women rated themselves as less satisfied, less committed, and
less close to their partner than their counterparts. If I could offer
one piece of advice when it comes to consumerism and dating,
it would be for people to spend less time trying to increase the
number of choices available and more time trying to enjoy those
they already have.

3 ½

The Dating Culture, Part II

What I Learned About Dating from Sex and the City

W HILE CONSUMERISM AFFLICTS ALL OF US, OUR CUL-
ture has changed in ways that, looked at from the standpoint of dating, is an ongoing disaster for women. Earlier chapters
focused on how evolution has shaped men and women to behave in certain ways, and almost all of that behavior qualified in
one way or another as politically incorrect, so it should not come
as a surprise when I say that feminism as a social and political
movement conflicts with some of the most basic and deep drives
of evolution. And because social and cultural change occurs
with lightning quickness when compared with biological evolution, man and woman as shaped by culture exist uneasily at best
with man and woman as shaped by evolution, leading to all sorts
of strange lacunae in the mating dance. I have to warn female
readers: The following pages are a grim catalog of how our culture is screwing with women.

WHY PRUDISH IS BETTER THAN SLUTTY

Let's look first at sex. By most accounts, feminism has made real strides in this area. And if the movement hasn't entirely knocked down boardroom doors, it has certainly done so with bedroom doors. Despite women's sexual liberation, though, the double standard persists. As anyone who has spent time in an American high school knows, boys who hook up a lot are still considered studs, while girls who do the same are still considered sluts. Even with all of feminism's advances, it sometimes seems as if the only two sexual positions for women are the Madonna or the whore. Obviously, these stark poles are a completely unrealistic picture of female sexuality, but this dichotomy may play a bigger role in our minds than we think. The world is a complex place, and scientists have found that all of us employ something called "heuristics," which is a fancy way of saying that we carry around a few simple rules in our heads that help us make many of our decisions. For example, when we taste something bitter, we spit it out. There are very good reasons for this. Many bitter foods are poisonous, and we probably evolved a dislike of bitter foods. But we don't go through this conscious thought process every time we eat. We don't consider each mouthful and weigh its various properties. That would be too time consuming. So, avoiding bitter foods acts as a simple heuristic to help us get on with the actual task of eating.

It is possible that the Madonna-whore distinction serves exactly the same function because it occurs in a number of different cultures around the world. All of us know that this dichotomy is an oversimplification, but I am talking about a level of thought that is below the chatter of our conscious minds. On this deeper level, the Madonna-whore divide serves as a simple heuristic for mating, and you can see the obvious advantages from the male point of view. In the first place, any sexually promiscuous woman is going to be a greater risk for a man when it comes to the task of determining paternity. But there is an even more fundamental reason that takes us all the way back to evolutionary fitness. Remember that the woman is the holder of the precious egg. By that logic, she should be quite choosy when it comes to selecting a mate. If she isn't, that sends a powerful message—that she is unable to secure a long-term mate and has decided to settle for whatever short-term relationship she can get. In evolutionary terms, she is sending a signal that she is not a particularly desirable mate. And my interviews with men confirmed that this signal comes through loud and clear. The quickest way for a woman to turn herself from a long-term prospect into a short-term hookup is to sleep with a man too soon. How soon is too soon? That's a little more vague, but if she wants to have a serious relationship, she should definitely prolong the period of waiting.

I know that on a conscious level all of this seems a little farfetched. But remember—heuristics are a way to help us simplify a complex world. To try to determine precisely the degree of promiscuity that is acceptable, by taking into account individual and societal factors, is an enormously difficult task. The Madonna-whore dichotomy is a way to cut through all of that and divide women quickly and easily into suitable and unsuitable mates. At the very least, women's sexual liberation has played a direct role in decreasing male commitment. According to a national marriage survey by

Rutgers University, the No. 1 reason men give for not committing to one woman is that they know they can get sex without marrying.

There's also another twist to this story, one that carries a pointed betrayal of sisterhood. It is quite possible that the currency of a term like slut is largely due to women, not men. A sexually promiscuous woman is, in many ways, a larger threat to women with partners than she is to men, because that sexual availability can lure away a boyfriend or a husband for a short-term or even a long-term relationship. The use of a term like slut is a way for women to police the sexual practices of other women and to convince men that certain women are to be avoided precisely because of how sexually available they are.

The obvious advice to take from this if you are a woman is that you should avoid having sex until a man is fully committed to you and that you should not offer your charms to many men. And many of the women I interviewed adopted precisely this strategy once they became more serious about finding a long-time partner. As one woman said, "You need to wait as long as possible. Once you have sex, you lose your uniqueness and become more of a commodity." Many of the women said that, paradoxically, the more that they like a man, the longer they make him wait before having sex.

But there are obvious drawbacks to this. In the first place, women enjoy sex just as much as men. In the second place, our culture has become so promiscuous that a policy of strict celibacy practiced by any individual woman is likely to keep men away as much as it attracts them. Perhaps the wise strategy is for women simply to increase the amount of time that must pass before they will have sex. With this in mind, I offer my completely unscientific and tongue-in-cheek rule to women trying to decide how long is long enough: double down! In other words, if you typically have sex on the third date, wait until the sixth date. If you typically wait four weeks, try to wait eight. Although this will involve some self-sacrifice in terms of short-term sexual pleasure, it will strengthen the signal that you are a high-quality woman who can afford to be selective about your sexual partners.

It is also worth considering the flip side of this, the stud. Academic studies and common sense both agree on a simple point: attractive men have more sexual partners than average men. Going back once again to our sperm/egg distinction, the reason why becomes obvious: women are willing to sacrifice long-term partnerships for good genes—and they do this quite knowingly. According to one study, women put more emphasis on a man's looks when they expect the relationship to be short term. For women interested in a relationship, the paradoxical advice is to avoid this type of man altogether. Even if you can convince such a man to commit to you, studies show that he is much more likely to be unfaithful. In other words, the term "stud" should worry women just as much as the term "slut."

HOW WOMEN CAN BE TOO SUCCESSFUL FOR THEIR OWN GOOD

Sex is not the only area where cultural feminism has run ahead of evolutionary biology. This tangled web has invaded our pocketbooks as well as our bedrooms. Remember that according to evolutionary psychologists women look both for good genes and good resources when selecting a mate. In our postfeminist world, though, more and more women are successfully pursuing high-powered careers and achieving economic success. Given this development, you would expect that these women would place much less emphasis on a man's resources and much more on his genetic quality. But culture changes much more rapidly than evolution. Nowhere is this more evident than in a successful woman's attitude toward how successful her future husband needs to be. It turns out that successful women don't place less importance on a man's financial success—they place *even more* emphasis on it. They still want the man to earn more than they do. In fact, injecting female success into relationships has added a new layer of instability. According to one study, when women earn more than their husbands, they are 50 percent more likely to get divorced than a couple in which the wife earns less, and divorce itself is closely linked with women's economic independence.

This is a problem that is only likely to worsen with time. One examination of the 2005 census data has revealed that women in their twenties earn higher salaries in several major cities than their male counterparts. The reason for this is largely due to education. Fifty-three percent of these women are college graduates versus only 38 percent of men—a double whammy for women from a dating perspective since, on average, men and women prefer for the man to have an equal or greater amount of education. According to a recent *New York Times* article, the salary differential has become a source of hostility between men and women, and many women now downplay their success, even as they still find themselves struggling to overcome their own expectations about men being the primary breadwinners.

All of these issues were regularly voiced by the women I interviewed. One woman said that she took her title off her e-mail to avoid intimidating men, while another said that she tried not to mention her degree from Wellesley because she didn't want to sound like "a Gloria Steinem type." Another made a point of emphasizing certain weaknesses, such as always joking about her inability to find her keys, as a way to come across as less intelligent. And a number of women hid the fact that they owned their apartments. Success at work also creates its own identity issues. A successful marketing executive said that she had problems when she would go out on a date directly from work. At work, she had a serious, no-nonsense attitude, and she would carry this attitude into the date, which immediately turned off most men who wanted to feel that they were in control. She kept hearing from mutual friends that the men found her "intimidating." She now goes home after work, changes clothes, and consciously tries to act more feminine and demure.

While men are hesitant to say that they are turned off by female success, most admit that it does play a role in their dating. All of the men I interviewed said that they did not like "hard-core feminists." Most also expressed doubts about a relationship in which the woman was more successful. Only a few men would say that they were actually threatened. Most preferred to couch their concern in a more oblique way by saying that it was a sign that the woman "didn't share my values" or "wouldn't be a good mother."

All of this reveals a gap that has opened up between the environment we were shaped for and the culture in which we now find ourselves. Common sense suggests that a successful working woman should be interested in a man's genes, not his salary. Not only does she not need the money, it could be argued that going after a very successful man is counterproductive for the relationship. At the very least, such a man is probably committed to his work in a way that will force the woman to make sacrifices in her own career and that two high-powered careers could very well place additional strains on the marriage. Despite that, nearly every woman I interviewed said that she would not go out with someone less successful than she was.

Of course, this is what happens when a culture of abundance runs into evolution based on scarcity. For most of our history, we have struggled to feed ourselves. But too few calories is no longer the problem. Too many calories is. We have been conditioned for hundreds of thousands of years to stock up on calories when they are available, which is a great strategy when you are grubbing in the dirt for food but is a big problem when the 7-Eleven is right around the corner. The same sort of thinking is at work when it comes to women and financial resources. Study after study has shown that after you get past the deprivations of poverty, more money does not do much to increase your happiness. In a study asking people to report how much of the time they were in a bad mood the previous day, people earning less than $20,000 clocked in only 12 percent higher than people earning more than $100,000, which is less than most of us would have guessed. But we are programmed to secure as many resources as we can, even if those come at the cost of our own happiness. If you don't believe me, let's try a little experiment. Imagine you are faced with two propositions. You can either earn $40,000 a year and live a very happy life, or you can earn $500,000 a year and live a mildly unhappy life. Which option is more appealing?

Most of us would be better off in our relationships if money played a smaller role in our decisions about which people we should date. Successful women, if they can overcome their natural prejudice, would especially benefit from looking for relationships with men who are less successful financially, and there are occasional glimmers of this, such as articles about white-collar women dating blue-collar men. The competition is less fierce for those men, and there is a very good chance that the man will devote more time and energy to the relationship than a high-powered careerist—if both partners can overcome their innate prejudices about who should bring home the bacon.

MEN DON'T MAKE PASSES AT WOMEN WHO WEAR GLASSES

Education for women has also been a mixed blessing when it comes to dating. I realize that one of the fundamental pillars of feminism is opening wide the doors of academia for women, and I support that. But it comes with a definite cost. In the first place, the more education a woman has, the older she is when she marries. On average, American women marry when they are twenty-five. If they have a college degree, that average rises to twenty-seven. A master's or professional degree lifts that to thirty. The reason this matters is because age is a crucial component of a woman's prospects. Men tend to marry younger women, so the older a woman gets, the smaller her dating pool becomes. In addition, education shrinks a woman's dating pool because men also tend to marry women with less education than they themselves have. Finally, intelligence itself appears to be a hindrance for women looking to marry. According to one study, women who had never married were much more intelligent than average—of course, feminists can claim that more intelligent women are too smart to fall for a patriarchal trap like marriage.

If you have any doubts about the larger cultural anxieties currently surrounding the dating scene for successful women, you only need to look at recent movies, which have offered a never-ending stream of stories about confident, capable women and the feckless men they are trying to shoehorn into marriage: *High Fidelity*, *About a Boy* (virtually the entire Nick Hornby oeuvre, in fact), *Old School*, *Failure to Launch*, *Knocked Up*, and *Wedding Crashers* just to name a few. Although the overt message of *Sex and the City* was that single, professional, successful women in New York City had sustaining friendships and exciting lives in which men were more accessory than essential, the implicit message was the opposite—that they desperately needed a man in their lives.

IT'S ALL IN THE NUMBERS

Of course, one key element is out of the control of men, women, culture, or evolution—demographics. Because, to some extent, it is all a question of numbers, and when you tally up the latest population figures, what you discover is that the odds are currently stacked against women when it comes to dating.

If you are old enough, you probably remember a famous article that *Newsweek* ran back in 1986, which reported that single women in their forties were more likely to be killed by a terrorist attack than to get married. What is particularly interesting about this bogus factoid is the willingness of so many of us to believe it for so long. Why would we be willing to accept something that should have sounded about as plausible as the idea of aliens abducting humans? The reason is that the theory spoke to a larger cultural anxiety. It may not have accurately described the situation, but for many single women it offered confirmation of what they were feeling at the time. And what they were feeling—without realizing it—was a massive demographic shift.

The women who found that statistic so plausible were the first generation of women to grow up after the feminist revolution. They were the proud inheritors of the right to work, and many of them pursued careers. But those careers came with a price. And that price was a shrinking dating pool.

The fear of a shortage of marriageable men has a long and proud history in our culture. Just think of all of the portrayals of spinsters, with their powerful reminders to women of what happens if they fail in the dating game, going all the way back to colonial times. Lest women think that their worries today are fundamentally different than those of some earlier golden age, such as the 1950s, they only need to read women's magazines from that period, which published articles on where to find eligible husbands and even ran data from the U.S. Census to determine which areas of the country had the most favorable ratios for women.

But the feminist revolution of the 1960s and 1970s accelerated certain demographic trends that significantly worsened the problem. With women pursuing careers, they were also marrying later, and this had profound repercussions because it ran into another trend that probably goes all the way back to our days on the grassy savannas—men tend to marry women younger than they are. According to studies, women look for men who are three and a half years older on average, while men prefer women roughly two and a half years younger. As we saw in the chapter on evolution, there is a fairly obvious reason for these preferences: men want access to women who can successfully reproduce, and so they seek out younger women. Women want men who can provide for them, so they seek out men who are older and more established. This is largely unconscious but no less potent because of that. And marriages do generally conform to these desires. In 1996, first-time brides were on average 24.8 years old, and first-time grooms were 27.1 years old.

All well and good, but that still doesn't explain why anyone found it even remotely plausible that a woman would have a greater chance of dying in a terrorist attack after the age of 40 than she would of marrying. To see why that struck some people as plausible, we have to consider the implication of this skewed age preference as it works over time. Because women prefer to marry someone older, their dating pool naturally shrinks with each passing year, while the dating pool of men expands with each year. In other words, men find their stock rising as dating prospects at precisely the moment that women find their stock falling. So, while the Enjoli perfume ad may have promised women that they could bring home the bacon and fry it up in a pan, it neglected to tell them that they might not have someone to cook for—namely, a man.

And age is not the only criteria that feminism has influenced. As I've discussed, men and woman also pay attention to things like education, income, and professional status. So, men tend to marry women who are younger, make less money, have less education, and are lower on the corporate ladder (there are many stories of male bosses marrying their secretaries, but I have yet to hear one about the female boss who married a male secretary). This is why the dating scene is not necessarily the friendliest place for successful, single women in their thirties or forties—and why that ridiculous terrorism statistic gained such widespread currency.

An added twist worsens this demographic trend for older women—age preferences do not remain stable. As men grow older, they are no longer satisfied with a woman only two to three years younger. They want a woman even younger. According to statistics taken from personal ads in newspapers, men in their thirties want a woman roughly five years younger, while men in their fifties want a woman ten to twenty years younger. Marriage statistics bear this out. For first marriages, American grooms are roughly three years older. By their second marriage, that number climbs to five years, and by third marriages men are on average eight years older.

What all this means is that the gains of feminism in the workplace are a double-edged sword. Although women are rising to ever-greater positions of power in corporations around the country, they are often putting their romantic lives on hold to do so.

Feminism has empowered women, but it has left them with a stark choice: improve their career prospects or improve their marriage prospects. If women really want the best partner, they should look for him when their stock is highest, while they are in their twenties. If enough women do this, there will also be fewer single women in their thirties, which would improve the dating situation for those women as well. Of course, early marriage comes with a career cost, particularly if marriage also leads to mother-hood. One ingenious economist has discovered that a woman in her twenties will increase her lifetime earnings by 10 percent if she delays the birth of her child by a year. That's *lifetime* earn-ings, not a 10 percent increase for one year but a 10 percent in-crease (on average) each and every year for the rest of her life, just for waiting an additional year to have a child. It's enough to make a Chia pet start to seem like a plausible alternative to children.

I consider myself a feminist, and I am certainly not trying to argue that women shouldn't pursue a career if that is what they want to do. But I don't think it serves anyone's interest to deny that a woman's career carries a romantic cost, particularly if her career delays her interest in marriage. If women can be honest with themselves about that cost from the start, then it may allevi-ate some of the angst that often afflicts so many single women in their thirties and forties.

None of this means that older women are doomed. These are only averages, and if averages told the whole story, we would all have 1.86 children. There are plenty of couples among whom the woman is the same age or older. But it does help to be aware of these preferences because when they are multiplied over entire populations, they can have enormous consequences. That's why the loudest complaints about dating usually are heard in large cities where these imbalances can be felt more powerfully (you could also argue that living in a large city is bad for a couple, regardless of any other factors. According to one study, proximity to many potential partners has a powerful effect on marriage and leads to more divorce even for couples who consider themselves happy).

Call it the multiplying power of small preferences. I live in

New York City, which is one of those places where the numbers are particularly hard on women. In Manhattan and the outer boroughs, there are roughly ninety men for every one hundred women. That ratio may not sound that bad. After all, it leaves us with just one female lonely heart for every eighteen contented people. But that ratio understates the case because many people are already in relationships of one sort or another, so 9:10 could turn out to be something like 4:5, in which case you've just doubled the number of lonely hearts and laid the groundwork for the popularity of a show like *Sex and the City*, which echoed the feelings of many professional women who had been told they could have it all but hadn't been told that there might be a price to pay.

How tough a town is New York for a single woman in her thirties? One British woman signed up for a slew of dating services, hoping to find a husband, and became so disheartened after two years of looking that she left the country and returned to Great Britain to look for a husband on native soil. And a number of women complained of the gross disparity in standards. While they were supposed to have all sorts of wonderful qualities, any man who was single, heterosexual, and had a job was considered a catch.

My interviews also revealed that for many men the demographic imbalance has made New York into a sexual Shangri-la (especially if they are reasonably successful). If I had to sum up in one word the attitude of a number of single men I interviewed, it would be "smug." Many of the men were uncomfortable even applying the word "dating" to what they were doing because that imposed too many constraints. They preferred to speak about "hanging out" and "hooking up," phrases too nebulous to be defined as anything implying commitment.

You don't need to look at a city-sized population to see how sensitive dating is to numbers. A study of speed daters turned up a similar effect. No matter how many people were participating on any given night, men's selectivity did not change. Bigger groups simply meant that they would ask out greater numbers of women. But women were highly sensitive to group size. When the groups were small (fewer than fifteen people), women were no more selective than men, but as the group size increased, so did the selectivity of the women.

Marcia Guttentag wrote an entire book about this, titled appropriately enough *Too Many Women?* Before World War II, there was always an excess of men, but the post-war decades have reversed that, providing a ratio of ninety-five men for one hundred women. As her work reveals, this small gap has surprisingly large consequences. Let's look at one representative year from her book. In 1970, among Americans fourteen years and older, there were ninety-two men for every one hundred women. That represented a surplus of roughly five million women. Once she removed married women from the count, though, the gap may have remained at five million, but the ratio significantly worsened, leaving only eighty-one men for every one hundred women. According to my own rough calculations based on the census data from 2006, there are approximately ninety-four men for every one hundred women today in America.

Of course, different demographic categories can have wildly different prospects. For instance, people tend to marry someone of their own race and ethnicity. For all white men and women between the ages of fifteen and forty-four, the ratio is a balanced one hundred three men for every one hundred women, based on the 2006 census, while the ratio of all black men to women from the ages of fifteen to forty-four is eighty-seven men for every one hundred women.

These skewed numbers don't simply have ramifications for a woman's ability to get a date. They also have a profound influence on society as a whole. As Guttentag realized, sex ratios shape sex roles. Looking at the historical record, Guttentag found that societies with more women than men shared a number of characteristics, such as a rise in illegitimate births and an increase in sexual libertarianism. Of course, none of this means that demographics is destiny. After all, no one marries .94 of a partner, even if our mates do sometimes fall short of our ideal.

THE CONSOLATIONS OF SINGLENESS— AT LEAST FOR WOMEN

But, single women, take heart! I also come with some very good news, which should liberate you from certain stereotypes with which you are bludgeoned. Even if demographics and our culture are working against you, the latest science reveals that it is men who should be far more worried about finding the right partner. All those jokes about inept bachelors living in a sinkhole of their own filth appear to contain some truth. You only need to take a look at average life expectancy for married men and women versus single men and women. To pick the starkest example, nine out of ten married men alive at forty-eight will still be alive at sixty-five. The corresponding rate for single men? Six out of ten (with divorced and widowed men faring only slightly better than confirmed bachelors). Not getting married is worse for a man than heart disease. While heart disease will shorten a man's life by a little under six years, not being married will shorten it by almost a decade. Women benefit from marriage as well. A nonmarried woman has a 50 percent higher rate of mortality. But men benefit far more—a nonmarried man has a mortality rate 250 percent higher. So, despite the cultural stereotypes, men seem to need marriage more than women do. You can see this by how eager each sex is to remarry. Men are four times more likely to remarry, and they remarry sooner as well, averaging only three years between wives compared to nine years for women.

When you look at more nebulous measures, such as life satisfaction, the contrast is also stark. While married men have greater life satisfaction than single men, the situation is reversed for women. Single women actually have greater life satisfaction than their married counterparts. One study has even identified a "happiness gap" that has opened up between men and women. In the early 1970s, surveys showed that women were slightly happier than men, but that situation is now reversed, leaving men as the happier sex. The reason for this is likely due to the incomplete gains of feminism. Since the 1960s, the amount of time men spend working has gone down, while the amount of time they spend relaxing has gone up. Meanwhile, woman may do less housework, but they have also added a great deal more paid work to their schedules. Forty years ago, women spent about two hours a day doing work they found unpleasant, about forty minutes more than men. Now, that gap has grown to ninety minutes. Perhaps never before has the old country and western lament about how hard it is to be a woman been more true.

Unfortunately, the idea that being single is worse for men than it is for women is rarely the message that our culture sends out to single women. Just think of our cultural stereotypes. A single woman is expected to sink gradually into the slough of despond, alone except for her cats. By contrast, a man alone still inspires—although to a lesser degree than he used to—thoughts of a swinging bachelor along the lines of George Clooney. Unsurprisingly, this causes a certain amount of defensiveness in single women. Maureen Dowd, a successful single woman if ever there was one, titled her most recent book *Are Men Necessary?* It is almost impossible to imagine a successful single man giving his book the title *Are Women Necessary?* You could argue that men are simply too egotistical to worry that much about the opposite sex. For example, Christopher Hitchens wrote a book entitled *God Is Not Great*, which, translated into Dowd's terms, could be called *Is God Necessary?* so men get to worry about God while women worry about men. In fact, there is a whole subgenre of advice books that reveal the pervasive anxiety of women through their very stridence. My personal favorite: *Why cucumbers are better than men.* These books are the result of the intense pressure that our society places on single women. This is hardly a new phenomenon. One theory behind the Salem witch trials is that they were largely caused by the fear of young women in Salem that they wouldn't be able to find husbands.

That the reality of single women is so severely at odds with the stereotypical perception does not lessen the difficulties of a woman who wants to live her life in defiance of the romantic story line. But I hope that this data at least relieves some of the pressure, because the truth is, based on the available statistics, women should worry a lot less about getting married, and men should worry a lot more.

4

The Dating Game

What I Learned About Dating from Adam Smith

THERE IS A PARLOR GAME I'VE INVENTED CALLED The Dating Game (patent pending). It's simple. Each life choice you make either increases or shrinks your potential dating pool. Let's take my own life as an example. I went to an Ivy League college. That's excellent news for my dating pool. Women tend to marry someone with as much or more education than they have, and I get an added bonus for going to a prestigious school. After a few years in journalism (subtract points for low-earning potential but add some back in for having an interesting job), I went back to school for an advanced degree, which turned out to be a mixed blessing. I should have increased my dating pool because I could add women with advanced degrees to the mix, except that I made a fatal miscalculation. I did not get an MBA or a law degree, two very dependable engines of economic success; instead, I earned a Ph.D. in history. The job prospects are not great for humanities Ph.D.s, and even if you get a job, you will never achieve great financial wealth, although you will live a very comfortable middle- to upper-middle-class life. Since economic resources play an outsized role in a man's desirability, that put a definite ceiling on my dating prospects.

After graduate school, I moved to New York City, which also had a mixed effect on my dating. On the one hand, New York has a great many men who are successful financially. I came for a high school teaching job, which put me at the lower end of professional salaries and also shrunk my dating pool by losing me the status points I might have had as a college professor. On the other hand, I did have demographics in my favor since New York has fewer men than women. Being in my midthirties also helped because, as you know from the last chapter, women tend to marry older men.

In the dating pool at this point, I was in reasonable shape, although hardly a blockbuster candidate. I had some of the things women look for (education, financial stability, no excessive problems with halitosis), but I fell short in one crucial area, financial success. My prospects were middling. In certain dating microclimates, such as a culture with a greater-than-average respect for education, I would probably have a better chance than in the population at large. So what happened? I won't keep you in suspense any longer about our hapless, overeducated hero. I am currently married. Interestingly, my wife is Korean American, so there are possibly cultural factors that have given her a greater respect for education than your typical American, although she seems thoroughly unimpressed with my advanced degree when it comes to the usual marital disagreements.

But things would have been much worse for me if I were a woman. As we've already seen, men tend not to marry a woman

with more education, so a Ph.D. would have been a real alba-
tross. Also, moving to New York would have been a lousy idea
because of the shortage of men. Finally, with each year I failed
to marry, a cruel mathematical logic would have been working
against me. As Andy, male Ph.D., each year that passed increased
my dating pool. But as Andi, female Ph.D., each year would
have shrunk the dating pool.

While I don't think that The Dating Game is going to turn
out to be the Monopoly of the twenty-first century, it does provide a valuable lesson about the way that dating itself is susceptible to a certain kind of market analysis in which you can predict
how each move in your life can increase or decrease your value.
Of course, no game can ever master the unpredictability of life.
As Andi, female Ph.D., I was perhaps destined to meet and marry
that sensitive male English Ph.D. who shared my love of Austen
and was happy to name our children after our favorite literary
characters (Chuzzlewit Trees practically rolls off the tongue).
But academic disciplines such as economics and game theory
allow us to consider dating in a rational and unsentimental light.
Needless to say, when you start talking about something like dating through the lens of the dismal science, you are about as far
from the romantic story line as it is possible to be.

Oddly enough, the whole idea for *Decoding Love* first began
to take shape when I was reading a book about economics—
more specifically, a chapter on how game theory is being used by
economists to run more effective auctions (that is, more effective
from the sellers' point of view since the new methods are all about
squeezing the maximum number of dollars from the buyers). As
I read about auctions, a question popped into my mind—why

couldn't you use game theory to help navigate the world of dating? *Decoding Love* has evolved a long way from that original question. But the core idea of whether or not science could provide better answers about the how and why of dating remained. And this chapter is my attempt to examine that question by using economics and game theory. Even if those two approaches offer no final answers, they can at least give us a clearer understanding of some of the forces at work.

WHY SCIENCE IS BETTER THAN SELF-HELP GUIDES

If you don't believe me, all we need to do is analyze a few dating books with the tools of economics to see that they are almost woefully simplistic. Take, for instance, that dating sensation of the 1990s, *The Rules*. As the title suggests, it contained a number of rules to guide women's behavior when they were dating, rules about how much to talk on the phone and when to go on a date and on and on. This book spawned an entire dating industry — *The Rules II, The Rules for Online Dating, The Rules for Marriage, The Rules Dating Journal.* Ironically, one of the authors ended up divorced, although, given divorce rates, I would argue that she was a victim of percentages, rather than a victim of her own rules. Looked at from the standpoint of economics, though, only one rule was at work — creating an artificial scarcity to drive up a woman's market price. All the rules were designed to make the woman less available to men, to create the sense that any time with her was something of great value. I'm not arguing against the

Gary Becker who wrote an article back in 1973 titled, "A Theory of Marriage: Part I" in the *Journal of Political Economy* (Part II was published the following year). He assumed that rational-minded daters would search for the most desirable mates, which led him to predict "positive associative matching" or, in plain English, the idea that men and women with roughly similar levels of desirability would pair off. This simple conclusion involved numerous equations and lots of math. Becker is, after all, a Nobel Prize winner, not just some loudmouth down at your local bar, and he won his Nobel for finding ways to apply economic analysis to all sorts of human behaviors not usually associated with economics, such as marriage. Unwittingly, Becker provided the first tentative hints of how to apply theory and mathematical rigor to the distinctly fuzzy world of male-female relationships, and that initial inquiry has spawned thousands of followers.

Before I dive into this world, though, I want to emphasize that while the mathematical analysis is valid, it can get pretty weird pretty fast. Economists are busy these days slapping values on all sorts of things that you probably thought were impossible to quantify. For example, if you increase the amount of sex you have from once a month to once a week, economists estimate that it has the same effect on your happiness as a $50,000 rise in your yearly income. Has "earning" an extra $50,000 a year ever sounded easier? Marriage is worth an extra $115,000. For a woman, semen is worth $1,500 because there are a variety of chemicals in it that boost a woman's mood when absorbed vaginally, and touch brings us an additional $26,000 in well-being by reducing stress levels and boosting our serotonin and dopamine levels. Economists have even put dollar figures on things like

orgasms ($7,000) and sweat ($15,500). Interesting? Yes. But all
of this is likely a classic example of the old saying about knowing
the price of everything and the value of nothing. A mathematician named Sergio Rinaldi has even developed equations to
quantify love. Sounds great, doesn't it? The mystery of love solved
with the precision of a mathematical formula. The mathemati-
cally inclined among you are probably already perking up and
thinking that all of your problems are over. Well, let me keep you
in suspense no longer. Here are the equations he developed:

$$\dot{x}_1\,(t) = -a_1\,x_1\,(t) + R_1\,(x_2\,(t)) + I_1(A_2),$$
$$\dot{x}_2\,(t) = -a_2\,x_2\,(t) + R_2\,(x_1\,(t)) + I_2(A_1).$$

Helpful? I didn't think so. The equations come from Clio Cresswell's *Mathematics and Sex*. Her book is filled with equations
like that and is quite an enjoyable read. The main thing it taught
me, though, was not that math can explain the mysteries of love
but that math itself is fairly mysterious for a layman like myself.
When it comes to remembering numbers, most of us are not
much more sophisticated than our ancestors on the savanna.
George Miller, a cognitive psychologist, wrote a famous essay in
1956 called "The Magical Number Seven." He found that most
of us can't hold more than about seven things in our short-term
memory at any one time. So, I offer this chapter to you with one
caveat. Take everything in it with a grain of salt. Will it contain
some interesting information? Yes. Should you take it all literally? No. While game theory and economics can provide incredibly powerful analytical tools for understanding dating, real life
can never be reduced to simple formulas.

LET'S MAKE A DEAL

With that said, let's see if we can't ferret out some useful ideas from the dismal science and its equally gloomy cousin, game theory. First of all, let's start with the idea of the "marriage market." We all like to believe that we fall in love with someone for individual and idiosyncratic reasons. It makes us feel much better about ourselves because we can imagine that we are not the sort of people who make cold-blooded decisions about relationships. It also makes us feel better about love by providing a far more uplifting conception of our relationships than the cold, hard logic of the marketplace. But there is good evidence that the dating world really does function as a market and an efficient one at that. Researchers can literally chart on a graph the values that people place on various qualities, and despite our complexities as individuals, most of dating can be boiled down to a stunningly simple list of attributes. In broad terms, a woman's market value is dependent on her fecundity and attractiveness, while men are judged based on their earning potential and their commitment. It may seem entirely too simplistic to reduce dating to these criteria. After all, each of us has many more individual preferences. In general, though, these few variables are the key determinants of market value. In one study of lonely hearts ads in four major newspapers, the ads offered a perfect confirmation of this market-based approach. The older the women were, the less demanding they became in their advertisements. The higher a woman rated herself in terms of attractiveness, the higher the demands she made in her ad. Men who claimed to have greater resources were also more demanding, while men with fewer resources offered more commitment. I don't think we go around with well-defined market values in our head as we search for a mate. But I do think that, over time, our dating experiences gives us a sense of our worth, and we naturally gravitate to people of similar market value. In other words, I'm not saying that we fall in love with someone just because we think we are getting fair value for our own appeal; rather, our sense of our own appeal predisposes us to fall in love with someone of similar market value.

Although most people I interviewed were understandably hesitant to confess to such crass calculations, almost everyone admitted that marketlike thinking shaped his or her own approach to dating whether that was by listening to a friend arguing "that you could do better" or not approaching someone because he or she was "out of my league." One woman even confessed that she made a regular assessment of the "breakup value" of the relationship after it ended. She would inventory all the gifts she had received, tote up their value, and decide if the compensation "had made it worth the effort or not."

Despite the stigma associated with a market-oriented approach, one woman was an exuberant practitioner of market-style negotiations when it came to dating. As an MBA student, she was given a certain number of points each semester to bid for a place in popular classes. One semester, she blew her entire allotment to get into a class on negotiation, which was either a sign of her passion for the subject or a recognition of an abject lack of negotiating skills. The next semester, she immediately used what she learned in her dating. She was taught to analyze what the best alternative was to what she was offering and then work to weaken that alternative at the same time that she strengthened her position. In her own case, she found herself interested in a man who already had a girlfriend. So, she set about pointing out all the ways that his current girlfriend fell short. To increase her own appeal, she engaged in a variety of tactics to make herself seem more desirable. She flirted with other men in front of him and talked to him about their interest in her. She also downplayed her own career ambitions, which she feared would be a stumbling block. Finally, after softening him up, she brought him to the table and negotiated explicitly with him, noting all the reasons a relationship with her would benefit him and putting the squeeze on him by saying that she was going to move on if he was not ready to commit. Romantic? No. Effective? Yes. They are currently dating. Regardless of whether or not they stay together, I think it is safe to say that she is a woman who will go far. I'm not suggesting that everyone should start treating dating like haggling for a used car, but I do hope you find it reasonably convincing that the principles of the market can be applied to the world of dating.

If you accept that the logic of the market also rules the dating world to some extent, you can map out all of your moves according to one simple guideline. Is this likely to increase or decrease my market value? As much as possible, you want to position yourself as an object of scarcity and value. This sounds stunningly simple, so much so that I almost feel I am insulting your intelligence to state it so baldly, but it is also stunning how often people act in ways contrary to this, such as inundating an ex with phone calls or e-mails.

You also need to be honest about your own sticker price. If you are rich and beautiful and talented and funny and kind, you have tremendous market value and can get just about everything you could possibly want in a mate. But what if you are only average or, worse, below average? As many studies have shown, we are very reluctant to admit that and usually inflate our market value to the detriment of our love lives. In a recent survey, fewer than 1 percent of people rated themselves as less attractive than average, which means that 49 percent of us are fooling ourselves. Unfortunately, the cruel logic of the market applies not only to others but to ourselves, and the sad truth is that almost all of us like to imagine that we are more of a catch than we actually are.

What if we could be brutally honest and admit our inadequacies? What should we do then? In the open market, how should we go about selecting a mate? One researcher decided to find out. He set up an experiment in which he created a "mating market." People were given a certain number of mating dollars to spend on the qualities they wanted in their partner. By giving some people tight budgets (in effect, giving them a low market value), he was able to find out what were the absolute necessities of mate choice and what were the luxuries. Women with small budgets spent their precious dollars on intelligence, money, work ethic, and a sense of humor. Men with only a few dollars proved to be much simpler creatures. They spent their money on physical attractiveness, which is something that women consider a luxury.

The real dating market is not as simple as the experiment, though, nor is it as straightforward as it was when Becker wrote his groundbreaking articles in the 1970s. It has become much larger and more complicated. There used to be all sorts of constraints—geographic, social, economic—that limited your dating choices at any one time to a relatively small set of people. Now, though, the Internet offers almost limitless choices unfettered by any of the usual restraints—what you might call the globalization of dating. As you'll remember from the last chapter, multiplying the number of choices is not necessarily a good thing, and according to one recent study, many people are finding this expanded market overwhelming. The authors of the study call it "the chaos of love."

This unfettered market has created entirely new problems. In the first place, you have a much greater chance of a mismatch than you did when your dating pool was a small town with local men or women you had known for years. We live in massive societies in which we are—wittingly and unwittingly—competing with friends from our own social circles, random passersby, waiters and waitresses, old flames from college, and so on. In the second place, people are becoming increasingly befuddled about their own criteria for selecting a partner. In many species, there is only one criteria that determines who will mate with whom. If you are a female lobster, you are looking for a male with big claws. If you are a female peacock, you are looking for a big tail on your bird. If you are a female sperm whale, you are looking for—well, who knows what female sperm whales want? But it's not that simple for us. Perhaps it once was. Back on the African savanna, there weren't many things to consider. Perhaps Moog was a good hunter, while Horg built great fires. Today, on the other hand, we face a virtually endless number of criteria. Is he funny? Does she like emo rock? Does he cook? Does she look too much like his ex? When anything is possible, it becomes less clear what is essential. In response to this complexity, people are increasingly turning to experts to help them. In fact, anyone who uses an Internet site's own selection formulas to find someone is, in effect, relying on an expert. Ironically, this turn to expertise has simply added a whole new layer of complexity and a greater loss of control.

TO VIEW YOUR PROFILE, CLICK HERE

Let's turn our attention for a few moments to Internet dating sites. Almost all of them are engaged in a race to come up with a system to figure out the mating market, and while they aspire to science, they are still closer to medieval alchemists than modern chemists. Seemingly every site has hired its own "love guru" and developed some sort of top secret algorithm for matching couples. Chemistry.com has Dr. Helen Fisher, who has come up with a modified version of the Myers-Briggs personality test (if you ever spent time in a career counseling office trying to figure out what to do with your life, you probably took some version of this). She has written a number of wonderful books on love, but as she would be the first to admit, she isn't even trained in this area— her degree is in anthropology. When Chemistry.com's Web site tried to claim that its algorithm was based on the latest science of attraction, eHarmony complained to the Better Business Bureau and forced them to remove the claim. Match.com has created Perfect Match with its attendant guru Dr. Pepper Schwartz (also the writer of a number of excellent books), who has come up

with the "Duet Total Compatibility System," a more complicated reworking of Myers-Briggs than Fisher's. The most complicated of all is on eHarmony, where hundreds of questions
measure people across twenty-nine core traits. And the mathematical formula that makes sense of all those traits? They guard
that as if it is the secret formula for Coca-Cola.

The first problem with all these sites is that while they may
claim to be scientifically based, none of them has yet to pass the
real test of science—peer review. In other words, it's not enough
to say that you have come up with a magic formula. You have to
submit your research in a forum where other scientists can judge
the validity of your claims. This may sound nitpicky, but it is the
bedrock of scientific inquiry. While many of these dating services
say that they intend to publish their results, talk is cheap. I guar-
antee you that if any of these sites had clear evidence of success,
they would rush to publicize it.

If you start examining these sites using mathematics, the problems run even deeper. Lori Gottlieb wrote a very funny article for
The Atlantic Monthly a few years ago in which she complained,
among other things, that she wasn't matched with a single person on eHarmony. Neil Clark, eHarmony's founder, cheerfully
explained that her problem was that she was too exceptional and
that eHarmony did a much better job of matching average people.
Of course, that answer makes one wonder what help, if any, these
dating sites provide. The vast majority of people fall within one
standard deviation of the statistical mean for virtually every trait,
so if you are average, it would be almost impossible not to match
you with similar people and also virtually impossible to figure
out if there was any validity to the matching system.

You might think that the way around this is to measure more traits. From this point of view, eHarmony's twenty-nine core traits look pretty good. It is reassuring to have a long list of questions about yourself and what you are looking for in a partner. You can carefully calibrate just how important ambition or sense of humor or kindness is. When you finally stop clicking with your mouse, it probably feels as if all you have to do is sit back and wait for the computer to spit out your true love. But a little mathematical analysis reveals a fatal flaw with multiplying the criteria. Unfortunately, the more qualities a dating questionnaire includes, the more unlikely it is that you will find anyone who matches you. Even if you limit the survey to include only six possible attributes, you only have a one in twenty-eight chance of finding a match. And it quickly gets much, much worse. With as few as ten attributes, it can become impossible to find a match in any meaningful sense of that word. Mathematicians call this the "curse of dimensionality," which basically means that the more dimensions you consider, the harder it becomes to find any concept of similarity that makes sense. That much data is simply open to too many possible interpretations. In other words, piling on lists of qualities doesn't help narrow the field. It makes it impossible to narrow it.

All of this is not to say that these dating sites don't successfully match many people. They undoubtedly do. What I am suggesting is that their success has little to do with their so-called scientific algorithms. If you match enough people, some of them are bound to end up together, regardless of what sorting system you use. As the most honest scientific advisers to these sites admit, this field is in its infancy, and no one has cracked the code yet.

premium. Once you look at the dating market in these terms, you can find good and bad deals all over the place. Take, for example, short men. Women place an enormous value on height. In a study of personal ads, 80 percent of the women said they wanted a man at least six feet tall. Women value it so much that they end up overvaluing it in market terms. In a recent study of online dating, researchers found that a 5'6" man needed to earn about $175,000 a year more than a six-foot man in order to overcome his height disadvantage. A different online study basically replicated these results, finding that a 5'8" man needed to earn $146,000 more than the average salary to attract the same women as a six-foot-tall man, while a five-foot man needed to earn a whopping $325,000 more than the average.

By any measure, women are wildly overpaying for these extra inches of height, asking for roughly $30,000 a year in salary for each *inch* they are giving up. It's enough to make you wonder why any man 5'11" and under isn't wearing lifts. There is no denying that height is what biologists call a fitness indicator, a sign of good genes and good health, and studies have shown that women attribute all sorts of excellent qualities to tall men based on their height. Other studies have shown that tall men do enjoy many societal advantages as well. For example, it's virtually impossible to become president of this country if you aren't tall. You have to go all the way back to the nineteenth century to find the last president who was of below-average height. Even so, it looks as if a certain amount of irrational exuberance has crept into women's valuation of men's physical stature. Compare, for example, how much a man's height is valued in the workplace. In one study of men's salaries, each inch of height for a man is worth less than six hundred dollars a year in salary. That's more than a $29,000 spread per inch between the value that the economic marketplace places on height and the value that women place on height, a classic example of a market imbalance ripe for exploitation.

If a woman wants to be really smart about it, she can squeeze out even more value from a short man. She just has to find a short man who was tall in high school. This is not the oxymoron it may at first appear. What she should look for is a man who had his growth spurt early, giving him a chance to tower over his peers before they surpassed him in later years. Why is this an advantage? It turns out that adolescent height is an excellent predictor of intelligence. In addition, the height advantage during those formative years gives the men greater self-esteem, which also increases their chances of success later in life. In fact, all those salary statistics don't hold up when it comes to men who were tall in high school but short later in life. Those short men earn more like a tall man, despite their stature. The reverse is also true—short men in high school earn less later in life even if they are tall—so, considered from an economic point of view, women should avoid those men.

It is even possible to date a short man who is perceived as a tall man. The combination of status, power, and height is so ingrained in all of us that short men with the first two assets will often be credited with the last as well. In one study, the same man was introduced as either a lowly student or an esteemed professor. Afterward, when the students were asked to estimate the man's height, they guessed that the professor was several inches taller than the student. So, in some cases, you can get all the advantages of dating a tall man, including the perception of those around you that you are dating a tall man, even though you are actually dating a short man. Where can you get a better deal than that?

Once you start looking, there are lots of niches that can be explored. For instance, if you are a white woman who is open to marrying someone of another race, you can also take advantage of a market imbalance. According to one study of online dating, an African-American man needs to earn an extra $154,000 a year above the average salary to equal the success with white women that a white man enjoys, while a Hispanic man must earn an additional $77,000. Asian men are selling at an even steeper discount. They must earn an additional $247,000 a year. Men are more rigid in this regard than women. According to the study, women can't compensate for racial or ethnic differences with higher salaries.

And we've already seen how men undervalue intelligent women, even though intelligence is one of the most precious genetic gifts we can pass on to our children. Men also shy away from women who make too much money, which is completely irrational from an economic standpoint. Similarly, men avoid dating women taller than themselves, even though a woman's height is also a sign of genetic fitness. Of course, to take advantages of these market imbalances, people will have to overcome their natural tendencies, which is no easy thing. A recent survey found that only 4 percent of women were open to the idea of dating a man shorter than they were. But if people can make it over that hurdle, there are plenty of bargains to be found in the dating market.

Needless to say, some qualities never sell at a discount. For example, if looks are important to you, you are going to have to pay up. Women are a little more flexible on this score and are willing to trade looks for financial resources. A man judged to be in the bottom 10 percent in terms of attractiveness needs to earn an additional $186,000 over and above the average salary to compensate for his unattractiveness. For an unattractive woman, though, the market is unforgiving. No level of income will raise her success to the level of a woman in the top 10 percent in terms of attractiveness. Unattractive people also get penalized in the workplace. Unattractive women earn 5 percent less in salary and unattractive men earn 10 percent less than their attractive counterparts, while beautiful people earn on average 5 percent more than the rest of us ordinary people. And one of the most straightforward ways for an overweight woman to boost her market value is to lose weight—she'll get an added benefit in the workplace, as well. Economists estimate that an extra sixty-five pounds costs a woman roughly 7 percent in salary.

Of course, exploiting undervalued areas of the dating market or avoiding overvalued areas is different than trying to beat the market, which is one thing that daters should avoid. If you consider dating as a market, the natural assumption is that you want to get a mate with the highest market value possible, but that isn't necessarily a good idea. Snaring a partner who is far more valuable than you are in market terms is a recipe for disaster in the long run. A variety of studies have shown that people who do find mates who are out of their league are also more likely to find that their partner will later desert them for someone of greater value. A relationship is not a one-time negotiation. If one partner feels they aren't getting adequate value in return, he or she always has the option to look somewhere else. So, caveat emptor! Even in relationships, a deal can be too good to be true.

There is evidence that women, if not men, are more sophisticated in their analysis of the dating market than one might expect. Given the market-driven and somewhat crass nature of my analysis, you would expect that every single man and woman would simply try to get the partner with the highest value. According to a new study, though, women actively avoid maximizing mate value. In the study, women were asked to choose men ranging from low attractiveness to high and from low financial success to high. Market logic dictates that the women should have chosen men who were both very attractive and very successful, but they avoided those men and preferred guys who qualified as very attractive but were only a medium on the financial success scale. When the researchers tried to understand this puzzling result, the only theory they came up with was that women were worried that attractive, successful men were more likely to cheat on them or to leave the relationship altogether.

All of us, often unwittingly, are responding to what economists would call market pressures, which brings us to perhaps the most dramatic lever women have to manipulate their market value—sex. Typically, men are much more eager for sex, so women hold a huge negotiating advantage before a couple consummates the relationship. Withholding sex for at least some period of time is one of the best ways for a woman to manipulate a man's perception of her market value, by convincing him that sexual intimacy with her is a rare privilege. It is also the single easiest strategy to convince a man to think of a woman as a long-term partner, rather than a short-term conquest. According to one unsurprising study, college men viewed women who were easy to get as desperate and possibly even diseased. Even in applying this tactic, though, there are some subtleties. Another study found that playing hard to get was very effective—if it was done in a targeted manner. Acting coy was not successful when women practiced it all the time, but it was a particularly good technique when it was combined with the pursuit of one person. By spurning others while actively showing interest in one man, a woman can effectively signal to that man that she will be faithful and that she is an excellent value on the marriage market.

Despite the hesitations many readers may naturally feel when asked to think about dating in market terms, it appears that Americans in general are more comfortable with the idea of a marriage market than one would expect for a culture so besotted with the romantic story line. What else would explain the proliferation of dating sites such as dateamillionaire.com? A recent poll asked people of median income (earning between $30,000 and $60,000 a year) if they would marry an average-looking person if that person had money. Two-thirds of the women and half of the men said they would be "very" or "extremely" willing to marry for the money for an average price of $1.5 million. Showing an acute sensitivity to the importance of age for their market value, the price at which women were willing to marry varied widely. Women in their twenties wanted $2.5 million, and women in their forties wanted $2.2 million, while women in their thirties lowered their price all the way to $1.1 million, which the pollsters suggested was due to the additional biological pressure on women in their thirties to have children. Men were willing to sell themselves for less, settling for an average of $1.2 million. This is perhaps an intuitive recognition of the Darwinian logic of cheap sperm and precious eggs. While you may be somewhat aghast at these cold, hard calculations, the study reveals that a price can be put on virtually anything, even your own betrothal.

THE GAME OF LOVE

The use of market-driven thinking is not the only way to apply mathematical rationality to the world of dating. Another area that has gained increasing prominence in understanding animal mating, including the human variety, is game theory. Nobel Prize–winning mathematician John Nash, the subject of the movie *A Beautiful Mind*, made his most important contributions in the area of game theory. He came up with something now known as the Nash equilibrium, which allowed game theory to be applied to a much wider variety of issues, including dating (although no one would get around to applying it to that until the last couple of decades).

Game theory is a branch of applied mathematics that was initially used primarily in fields like economics and political science. There are a huge variety of "games" that one can play—zero sum and nonzero sum, symmetric and asymmetric, continuous and noncontinuous, cooperative and noncooperative, simultaneous and sequential to name just a few variations—but we're not going to worry about those complexities; instead, we're going to explore only a few areas where game theory might actually offer some practical assistance when it comes to dating.

First, some good news for women. They set the ground rules for the game. As I hope the chapter on evolutionary psychology proved, men want to have sex, and in general they want to have it more often than women do. Because of this, women are in the driver's seat. Game theory can demonstrate this through an examination of a question we explored earlier: why monogamy? Using the techniques of game theory, biologists have been able to reduce that complicated question to four linked propositions that determine whether a society will be monogamous or polygamous. Without further ado, a quick and dirty guide to the mating game, compliments of Matt Ridley's wonderful book on sex and evolution, *The Red Queen*:

1. If females are in a better situation by choosing a monogamous relationship, a monogamous society will be the result;

2. UNLESS men can force women into polygamous relationships (the "grabbing the woman by her hair and dragging her back to the cave" school of dating);

3. If females are not in a worse situation by choosing men already paired with a woman, a polygamous society will be the result (the "it's better to be the second wife of Brad Pitt than the first wife of Homer Simpson" school of dating);

4. UNLESS the females with mates can prevent their mates from adding an additional mate (the "don't touch my man, or I'll rip off your hair extensions" school of dating).

Did you see the role that men played in all of that? You have to look closely—male agency makes a brief appearance in proposition #2. Other than that, it's girl power.

Of course, we already know that we live in a monogamous society, and all sorts of variables creep in that quickly complicate any simple scenario. Take, for instance, the issue of sex. Women willing to accept a short-term relationship can probably attract a much higher quality mate than if they hold out for a long-term commitment. But a single woman can't completely alter her market value simply by withholding sex, because she is not only trying to attract a man but is also competing against other women.

Another classic game can illustrate the problems that this sexual uncertainty adds to the equation. Imagine that a group of hunters are chasing a stag. If they all work together, they will kill the stag and share in a vast quantity of meat. But there is a chance that they will fail to catch the stag. Then, no one will eat. A hunter can also desert the stag hunt and kill a rabbit. If he defects early, he has an excellent chance of killing one, although it won't be the meat bonanza of the stag hunt. If enough hunters defect, the stag will definitely escape, and only those early defectors who went after the rabbits will eat. The game outlines the difficulties of cooperation.

Now, imagine a similar situation with women who are all pursuing a high-status male with little interest in a long-term commitment. Only these women face an added difficulty—they will not share in the spoils of the hunt, which makes cooperation among them virtually impossible. If they all agreed to abstain from sex with him, they could very likely force him to choose a long-term partner. But some of those women will know that they are unlikely to win the prize. They might be happy to have a short-term liaison with the man (the equivalent of going after a rabbit), rather than nothing at all. So, while a woman can exercise great power over her suitors by withholding sex, she is not doing this in a vacuum, and there are plenty of women around her who will choose to play the game differently.

GETTING INTO THE GAME

As with analyzing dating as a market, people must first accept that there is an element of strategy in their own dating—another direct blow to the romantic story line, which insists that love is spontaneous and largely impervious to manipulation. Some people are reading this now and thinking, "I don't play games." You may very well believe this is true, but that is simply one more move that one can make in any game situation. By saying you don't play games, you are signaling to others that you have certain traits (trustworthiness, sincerity, etc.) that make you more attractive. You may also be trying to rule some games out of bounds (for example, you may be signaling that you won't tolerate deception). However, all but the most obtuse among us will admit that there are certain moves in the game of dating that we don't make, no matter how much we claim not to believe in games. For example, no one wants to look desperate. We all know that on a first date, no matter how well it is going, we don't blurt out that we think we might be falling in love or that the other person is "the one," even if we have glancing thoughts in that direction. It's a supremely bad move, more likely to signal that you are not a valuable dating partner.

There are an almost infinite number of moves in any encounter, but some basic ones frequently come into play. Men tend to deceive women about how committed they are, and women try to counteract that by imposing courtship costs. Some women even resort to what a game theorist would call the ultimatum game when they tell their partners that they have to be married (or engaged) by a certain date, or the relationship is over. Others try to impose strict rules for the games that are allowed by joining dating sites that have values built in, such as conservadate.com or singleswithscruples.com (which explicitly markets itself to people who are "tired of games"!).

My own personal favorite is the self-deprecation gambit. The appeal of the anti-appeal. In other words, you are such an attractive candidate that you can dispense with all the usual self-marketing, actively denigrate yourself, and still appeal to the opposite sex. This is more common that you might think. Just take a look at *They Call Me Naughty Lola,* a hilarious book on the self-immolating personal ads people have placed through the years in the *London Review of Books.* A few choice examples:

"Shy, ugly man, fond of extended periods of self-pity, middle-aged, flatulent, and overweight, seeks the impossible."

"Blah, blah, whatever. Indifferent woman. Go ahead and write."

"Unashamed triumphalist male for the past forty-six years.
Will I bore you? Probably. Do I care? Probably not."

Not only hilarious, they illustrate Zahavi's concept of the high-cost signal from the chapter on evolution. Only people with charm and looks and talent to burn (as well as excellent senses of humor) can afford to be so self-deprecating about themselves — which is a useful lesson for the rest of us: the soft sell is more effective than the hard sell.

For those interested in cleaning up the game of love, one simple change can help eliminate a great deal of bad behavior: increase the length of the game. That's what a political scientist did when he invited experts in game theory to submit computer programs to play against one another in a game known as the prisoner's dilemma. Several dozen programs were submitted, and they "played" for hundreds of rounds. The winner? The shortest program submitted — a mere five lines — which its creator dubbed "Tit for Tat." The program did exactly what you would expect. In its initial encounter with any program, it would cooperate. In all future encounters, it would do what the other program had done in the previous encounter. If the other program cooperated, it would cooperate. If the other program acted selfishly, "Tit for Tat" would behave selfishly. This simple idea of rewarding good behavior and punishing bad behavior bested every other program. To create a similar situation in the dating world, though, you would need to have the same two people "play" (i.e., date) each other multiple times. Under these conditions, people would quickly clean up their behavior because deception and other bad behavior would simply be punished in the next round.

Unfortunately, dating is not like that. The partners in any game are constantly shifting. But you could still achieve similar results if you had good enough communication. When people can communicate the past behavior of others, they can form networks of trust and shut out players who rely on deception. Imagine if each of us was given a rating based on our dating histories, similar to the buyer and seller ratings on eBay. If someone behaved badly, he or she would find it increasingly difficult to find anyone to date. When people lived in one place for most of their lives, gossip essentially served this function and helped impose a standard of behavior, and some Internet sites are now starting to adopt this concept, although it is far from foolproof since users can simply move to a new site. If one dating Web site ever dominates the way that eBay does with online auctions, it will have the power to improve the behavior (or at least the honesty) of men and women when they date—more so than anything since Moses came down with the Ten Commandments.

THE DOWRY GAME

While all this game theory may be interesting, some of you are probably wondering right about now, so what? Is there some more practical advice that game theory can offer? Well, yes, actually there is. For example, it can finally provide an answer to that age-old question: how many people do you have to date before you meet your true love? The answer: twelve. That's right. A nice, round dozen. Not too difficult, right? Okay, yes, I realize you are going to need more convincing than that. Many of you have dated far more than twelve people and are still no closer to finding a partner than you were when you were the age of twelve. Others are probably outraged that I would even put a definitive number on such an amorphous task. Besides, what's so special about the number twelve? It's not as if Cinderella crossed that threshold, which, by the way, is one of my pet peeves with the romantic story line. The storybook lovers always seem to meet the right person very early on, leaving the rest of us poor schlubs feeling that taking a long time to find love is itself another sign of failure.

But back to the lucky number twelve. How in the world can we possibly arrive at such a precise number? To understand that, I'm going to ask you to play a game. Mathematicians have called this game by a variety of names. We are going to play the version known as the dowry problem. Let me set the scene. You are the king's most trusted adviser. He wants to find you a lovely bride (or groom), but he also wants to make sure that you truly are as wise as he thinks you are. So, he arranges a challenge for you. He sends out his minions and finds one hundred of the most beautiful women in the land. He then provides each of them with a dowry, only he doesn't provide them with the same dowry. Each woman has a dowry different in value from all the other women. Your challenge is to pick the woman with the highest dowry. If you succeed, the beautiful bride and the sumptuous dowry are yours to enjoy, and your place at the king's side is secure. If you fail, he's going to chop your head off. Oh, and one more thing, you meet the women one at a time, and once you have dismissed a woman, you can never call her back. Ready? Let's play.

Being the brilliant adviser that you are, you probably have already figured out the math for all of this. I, of course, am terrible at math and am relying entirely on the excellent article by Peter F. Todd and Geoffrey F. Miller called "From Pride and Prejudice to Persuasion: Satisficing in Mate Search," which can be found in *Simple Heuristics That Make Us Smart*. Once you crunch the numbers, you realize that your best chance is to pass on the first thirty-seven women and then pick the next woman who has a higher dowry than any of the women who came before her. Mathematicians have dubbed this rather obviously the "37 percent rule." By seeing the first thirty-seven women, you will give yourself a 37 percent chance of choosing the highest dowry. Not the greatest of odds when you are under the threat of having your head chopped off but a better percentage than you will get with any other number. If the king lets you play the field a little bit, you can improve your chances dramatically. If you can keep one woman while you continue your search, you can increase your odds of finding the best dowry to 60 percent. Not too shabby.

Those of you who feel a little letdown about the 37 percent rule, raise your hands. Thirty-seven is nowhere near the twelve I promised. Dating thirty-seven people sounds exhausting. Well, apparently Todd and Miller agreed with you, and they set about tweaking the game in various ways to see if they could find a better way.

Instead of the 37 percent rule, you could try the "Take the next best" strategy. Of course, you are going to have to give up on the idea of "the one." If your sole criteria is trying to find the single-best mate, you've got to stick with the 37 percent rule. But if you are willing to accept anyone in the top 10 percent, you can follow the 14 percent rule. This rule works as you might expect. You pass on the first fourteen women (or men) and then choose the next woman who is better than those first fourteen. If you do this, you have an 83 percent chance of ending up with someone in the top 10 percent. If you are willing to accept anyone in the top 25 percent, you only need to look at the first seven women and then choose to have a 92 percent chance of success. Let's say you are unlucky in love and just want to avoid marrying someone in the bottom 25 percent. Then you only need to check out three women, and you will have less than a 1 percent chance of ending up with a loser. That may not sound all that great, but the 3 percent strategy still does a better job of avoiding losers than the 37 percent rule, which has a 9 percent chance of landing you with someone in the bottom 25 percent. While the 37 percent rule provides the best chance of picking the best person, it does worse at almost everything else, including picking someone in the top 10 percent or even the top 25 percent. It also results in a lower overall average mate value.

Running all the numbers, it turns out that the best strategy is the 10 percent rule, which results in the highest average mate value, a high chance of landing someone in the top 10 percent and a very high chance of landing someone in the top 25 percent. To give you some sense of how much more effective the 10 percent rule is than the 37 percent rule, compare the average mate values. The 10 percent rule gives you an average mate value of 92 out of 100 versus an average mate value of 81 out of 100 if you use the 37 percent rule (and you have to date a lot fewer people!). The 10 percent rule isn't particularly onerous. You only need to date ten people from a field of one hundred. That is lower than the twelve I originally promised. Of course, you are likely going to have to date more than just those ten. Remember the way the game works. The 10 percent rule means that you have to pass on the first ten people and then choose the next person who comes along and is better than the first ten. On average, you will end up working your way through roughly thirty-four potential candidates.

Of course, there are probably some indefatigable daters out there who think that one hundred people is a rather paltry total: the dating decathletes among us who are perfectly happy to date one thousand people if it improves their chances of finding true love. If you are choosing among one thousand women (or men), the 37 percent rule means that you will no longer be doing anything but dating for the foreseeable future. If you are willing to accept someone in the top 10 percent, though, you only need to apply the 3 percent rule for a 97 percent chance of success. And the numbers are even better if you are willing to accept someone in the top 25 percent. After running the game for numbers ranging from one hundred to several thousand, it all boiled down to one simple rule: try a dozen (Cresswell dubbed this the twelve-bonk rule, bonk being a British word for . . . well, I'm sure we all know what bonk means). Todd and Miller found that this number provided excellent results no matter how large the sample size. As they aptly put it, "A little search goes a long way." We may still choose the wrong person, but the "try a dozen" rule shows that our mistakes are probably not from lack of trying.

Although I have yet to meet anyone who has explicitly used the twelve-bonk rule to choose a partner, the anecdotal evidence suggests that some of us subconsciously follow a method roughly analogous to it. For example, a number of people said that they viewed finding the right person as a simple numbers game. They just had to ensure that they met enough people in order to find the right fit. I realize this contradicts to some extent what I said earlier about too much choice, but it is very different to date several dozen people over the course of several years than it is to scan hundreds or even thousands of online profiles in the course of a few hours. The surprising thing was how often the numbers roughly correlated with what the twelve-bonk rule predicts. One woman decided to get serious about meeting someone and went on thirty-eight dates over a two-year period before finding Mr. Right, which is very close to the average predicted by the "try a dozen" rule. Another woman inadvertently ran her own modified version of the dowry game, albeit without the fatal consequences. She went on a hundred first dates, ruthlessly culled from that list ten men for a second date, ruthlessly culled again and went on a third date with three men. She ended up having a long-term relationship with two of the men, and she married one of them. I also found a variety of other people who had used methods roughly analogous to game theory. One systems engineer even described his marriage as a "system deployment," a statement that positively drips with romance.

Of course, life is never so simple. There are numerous ways that the dowry game does not reflect real life, although it would be nice to lie on plush cushions, eat grapes, and wait for beautiful women to be brought to you. We are going to focus on the most important one: mutual choice. The dowry game assumes that you simply get to choose whichever woman (or man) you want. What it fails to recognize is that in our society, the women (and men) also exercise their own choice. They are perfectly free to look at your lazy, grape-eating ass and decide to marry that ruggedly handsome camel trader back in their hometown.

Miller and Todd ran the game again with one hundred men and one hundred women, and they found that the more possible partners both sexes checked out, the lower the rate of people who ended up in a relationship. The reason was that people began setting their aspiration level too high. You may set your sights on a woman in the top 10 percent, but if you are in the bottom 25 percent, you are going to end up single. For people to find their way into a relationship, a new element needed to be added: people had to adjust their aspiration level based on the feedback they were getting. A great deal of math is involved, and Miller and Todd experimented with a number of scenarios on how to determine mate value. To put it in simple terms, if you use the twelve-bonk rule, your expectations are likely going to be too high.

It is also important to remember that many aspects of dating are not susceptible to mathematical analysis. For instance, women would find it very useful to know the ratio of men who are likely to be loyal partners versus those who will cheat. Unfortunately, there is no definitive answer to this question, for the simple reason that the ratio will change depending on the social environment. The best strategy for men is mixed. In other words, depending on the context, it may make sense for a man to be faithful, or it may make sense to pursue opportunistic sex. Game theory itself predicts that players will cultivate unpredictability as a way to avoid being easily manipulated in the game.

Worse, it is quite possible that the players might not even be aware of their own gamesmanship. Our old friend Trivers of the parental investment theory has called this "adaptive self-deception." If you buy this theory—and anyone who has listened to a friend justify some completely preposterous course of action will—we are so good at deception that we often manage to deceive ourselves as well. This self-deception is incredibly useful to us from an evolutionary standpoint because successfully masking our intentions from ourselves makes it much more likely that we will also deceive those around us. You can see the benefit of this in a host of situations. Just think of a single man on the prowl for a one-night stand. He might meet a woman in a bar and immediately become convinced that she is the love of his life. He woos her intensely and is able to look her in the eye and tell her with great sincerity that he thinks she is far more than some easy sexual conquest for him. Because of this, he convinces her to spend the night with him. When he wakes up in the morning, he realizes that he was deceiving himself the entire time. In the cold light of day, he knows that he has no interest in a long-term relationship with the woman, but his self-deception has already served the purpose that evolution designed it to serve—to spread his genetic material.

ENDGAME

Although amusing to examine dating using economics and game theory, these approaches are limited by their failure to account for the irrationality that guides so much of our behavior, particularly when it comes to love. To see this, let's play a game called How Much Would You Pay For a Dollar? I don't think it takes a mathematical genius to determine that you should pay no more than ninety-nine cents. What if a wrinkle is added, though, and the second-highest bidder also has to pay his bid, even though he has lost the auction? Now, how much should you pay?

That's exactly the game that Martin Shubik, an economist, played a number of times with different groups of friends. As he wrote in his article, the game is ideally played under what might be called boisterous conditions: "A large crowd is desirable. Furthermore, experience has indicated that the best time is during a party when spirits are high and the propensity to calculate does not settle in until at least two bids have been made." Shubik identified three crucial points in the game. The first was whether two people were willing to make a bid. The second crucial moment came at fifty cents when the people bidding realized that any higher bids meant that the auctioneer would make a profit. And the third crucial point was at one hundred cents when someone had, in effect, offered to give a dollar to get a dollar. At this point, his opponent would already be committed to pay his own bid and usually decided to bid $1.01. Even though he would be giving more than the dollar was worth, he would at least get the dollar and only lose one cent, rather than the value of his entire bid if he lost the auction. Once a player bid more than one dollar in order to receive one dollar, the bidding tended to escalate rapidly. Shubik kept track of the results and found that, on average, the dollar bill sold for $3.40. Since Shubik also kept the losing bid, he took in over six dollars and had to pay out only one dollar. Some of the games were even more extreme. One "winner" ended up paying twenty dollars for the dollar and only succeeded with that bid because his opponent ran out of money. On another occasion, a husband and wife bid against each other and were so upset by the experience that they went home in separate cabs.

Since then, the same game has been run in a number of research labs with the same results. In one test, more than forty groups were studied, and in each and every case the group went over the one-dollar mark. Half the time the bidding only stopped when one of the players had offered all his money and couldn't bid anymore. Researchers also found that people rarely learned from their mistakes and that even players who had already engaged in the game would usually still end up bidding more than a dollar. What makes this especially striking is that the item being bid for—one dollar—has a precise value. There can be no confusion about what it is worth. Even the slowest of players realizes that bidding more than a dollar to win a dollar makes no sense. When researchers tried to understand why people continued to bid, they found that it wasn't an economic calculation but an emotional one. Sure, when players started the game, they said that they were bidding primarily to win money. As the bidding moved higher, though, they changed their answers and claimed that they were doing it to prove a point, making such obviously self-defeating remarks as, "I won't be made a fool of." Although all of us are probably snickering at the fool who paid twenty dollars, the evidence suggests that we would be equally foolish.

Shubik's game is not simply a parlor trick but offers an excellent way to look at the problem of escalation. You can find examples of it throughout the real world. For example, Lyndon Johnson's rhetoric about the Vietnam War changed dramatically between 1964 and 1968. At first, Johnson emphasized democracy, freedom, and justice. Later, though, he spoke about national honor and avoiding the appearance of weakness, which as game theorist Laszlo Mero noted in his excellent discussion of the dollar auction from which this is drawn, "is strangely similar to the changes in motivation expressed in the dollar auction game."

This conundrum is even useful in understanding our everyday lives. If you have ever been in a hurry to get somewhere and were waiting for a bus, you have probably experienced a dollar auction situation. You may be debating whether or not to take a cab, and in fact if you walk to the bus stop and don't see a bus, you may just hop in a cab. The longer you wait, though, the more likely you are to continue waiting because you feel as if you have already invested all that time in waiting for the bus. Although we don't realize it, we engage in self-defeating dollar auctions all the time. Mero writes, "The principle of the dollar auction keeps many people in unsatisfying jobs and unhappy marriages."

What does all this have to do with dating? Quite a lot, actually. Take the animal kingdom. There are regularly situations when two males come into conflict over a female or a good mating territory. Some species fight, but others choose not to for a variety of reasons. For example, they may have particularly dangerous weapons, and a fight would possibly be fatal. In these cases, the animals often resort to something called "posing." Basically, they stand there and eyeball each other to see who wants it more and is willing to wait longer. In other words, a classic dollar auction situation. How do they solve this? As we've already seen, humans are not very good at escaping dollar auctions. We tend to empty out our pockets and throw everything we can at winning the auction. According to the mathematicians, the animals should assign a value for whatever it is they are fighting over and then choose to pose for a random amount of time based on that number. For example, if one of the males decides that the female is worth twenty minutes of his time, he should pose for some random variation between, say, twelve minutes and twenty-eight minutes. If he wins, great. If not, he simply walks away when he reaches his limit. When actual animals in the wild were studied, it turned out that they followed precisely this logic. In other words, most animals act much more rationally in this sort of situation than one particular kind of animal, human beings.

If we keep this in mind, it might help end a lot of suffering and misery for ourselves as daters, although it will mean that we have to give up some cherished romantic notions, which tend to land people in dollar-auction situations. For example, take the idea of unrequited love. The romantic story line tells us that a lover's constancy and persistence will ultimately be rewarded when the beloved finally recognizes his or her worth, but that is exactly the kind of thinking that can lead to a dollar auction. The more time that passes, the more the lover insists that there must be some sort of reward for all of his or her effort. And being in a relationship is also no protection against fruitless dollar auctions. Once you have been with someone long enough, you may avoid breaking off a relationship, even if you find it unsatisfying, because of all the time you've already invested. In fact, it's probably safe to say that anyone who has much dating experience has unwittingly found himself or herself in a dollar auction at some point. If I could leave you with only one piece of advice from this chapter, it would be to avoid dollar auctions when dating. If you can't avoid them, at least determine the price you are willing to pay beforehand so you know when to get out. Easier said than done, but no one ever promised that love was easy.

The Dating Dance

What I Learned About Dating from Hanging Out in Bars

WE'VE FINALLY REACHED THE POINT WHERE THE RUB-
ber meets the road, that electric moment when someone
catches your eye across a crowded room, and you know that you
are going to spend the rest of your life together. At least, that's
what the romantic story line tells us. In truth, much as you would
expect given the earlier chapters, you can do a remarkable number of things to enhance or detract from your appeal during your
initial encounter with your Romeo or Juliet.

Part of this chapter falls under a category that could be la-
beled "tricks" because it includes various methods to manipulate
someone's perception of you. I offer these "tricks" with a certain
amount of hesitation. It's not that I don't think they will work—
it's that I think they might work too well. My intention throughout *Decoding Love* is to try to understand the secret springs of
romantic attraction, not to provide a grab bag of techniques for
getting what we want at other people's expense. Just because the

Machiavellian theory of the mind suggests that we have a tendency to deceive, that doesn't mean we shouldn't struggle to rise above our baser instincts and embrace what James Madison called the better angels of our nature.

LET ME HEAR YOUR BODY TALK

With that said, let's return to the crowded room and look at what happens on some enchanted evening. The first important point to realize is that only a small part of what you are communicating at any moment is coming from the actual words you are saying. There are three ways that we are constantly sending out messages to those around us: body language, tone of voice, and actual words. Of course, if you are explaining a dense mathematical problem, the vast bulk of your communication will be carried by your words, but most of our communication is not like that, especially when it comes to dating. In most casual conversations, what we say is the least important of the three aspects of communication. I have read varying estimates, but roughly speaking, the vast majority of our communication comes from body language and tone, while less than 10 percent of our communication is the words we speak. So, what you say is far less important than how you say it. In one study, college students were hooked up to a portable tape machine that recorded random samples of their conversations throughout the day. When the researchers analyzed the data, they found that even those small snippets were "saturated with unintentional messages." We may not realize it, but in virtually all of our encounters, a vast sea of unspoken messages are passing back and forth, usually below our conscious notice.

All of this is doubly true for the world of dating where almost everything is done through oblique signals, rather than direct conversation. If you don't believe me, let's imagine a few scenarios. What would happen if a guy went up to a woman and told her that he found her incredibly attractive and wanted to sleep with her? If he was Brad Pitt, that might work. For most of us, though, that sort of direct approach would be a disaster. Or think how men would respond to a woman whose first question was how much money they made? Part of the reason for this is that these approaches don't pay the necessary lip service to the romantic story line, which drills into us the idea that there should be some deep, innate attraction that can't be explained by superficial external factors like a salary. This controlling myth is why dating is all about sending and receiving indirect verbal and nonverbal messages. For example, if you are a man and want to show off your financial success, don't brag about the size of your bank account. Show it off through your mastery of the wine list or some other realm that more subtly advertises your success. Indirect signaling is so important that the single easiest way to improve your romantic life is to become better at reading the signals that other people are sending out and better at controlling your own signals. This chapter will, I hope, help you figure out how to do that.

If you don't believe me, you simply need to look at a recent study of lap dancers by evolutionary psychologist Geoffrey Miller and his assistant to see how our actions are drenched with messages of which we are completely unaware. It is safe to assume that a lap dancer is always going to try to appear as sexy and attractive as possible because doing so has a major effect on the tips she will receive. What Miller's study found was that the amount of tips women received varied widely. And the variation wasn't random. It was tied directly to the fertility cycle of the women. A menstruating lap dancer made on average thirty-five dollars an hour, and a woman who was neither ovulating nor menstruating averaged fifty dollars. During their fertile periods, though, lap dancers were like Bathsheba on ecstasy, averaging a whopping seventy dollars an hour, double the menstruating women. The researchers have speculated that men were responding to a variety of subtle cues, such as body odor and waist-to-hip ratio, but regardless of the cause, it is stunning evidence of the power of the unintentional signal.

Most of the women reading this book are not lap dancers, but researchers have found that fertility has a number of similar effects on women in general. For example, men looked at pictures of the same women when they were ovulating and when they were not ovulating and rated them as more attractive during their ovulation. As with Miller's study, researchers are not entirely sure why this is the case. They think that men are responding to subtle cues related to things like lip color, pupil dilation, and skin tone. A woman's fertility cycle also appears to alter *her* behavior. For example, researchers have found that women dress more provocatively and wear more jewelry during ovulation. Another study revealed that ovulating women send out more signals to attract men than their nonovulating counterparts. Ovulation even appears to influence a woman's voice. In a recent study, men and women listened to recordings of women's voices at different periods in their fertility cycles, and researchers found that women at their peak fertility were judged to have the most attractive voices. So, it turns out that women who want to get pregnant are not the only ones who should keep track of their ovulation cycle. Any woman who wants to meet a man should do the same and, at the very least, try to schedule dates during her days of peak fertility. One other piece of advice if you are a lap dancer or just trying to meet someone: being on the pill comes with a cost. According to the study, lap dancers on the pill averaged only thirty-seven dollars an hour (hardly different from menstruating women), while women not on the pill averaged fifty-three dollars. With a difference that stark, you can be sure that the pill has a similar effect on the appeal of women in general.

LADIES' NIGHT

Even if most of us aren't lap dancers, virtually all of us have spent some time in the belly of the beast: the bar scene, which has been the site of far more research than you might imagine. That's right. Even the humble bar is a site of scientific interest—seedbed of bad pickup lines, drunken one-night stands, and even the occasional long-term romance. But not as far removed from the earlier chapters in this book as you might imagine. Think all the way back to the section on the precious egg and the profligate sperm. The same logic still applies, which means, for all of you astute evolutionary psychologists out there, that women are far more in control in this arena than it might appear. So, you can jettison all those cultural stereotypes about men being the aggressors and women being their passive playthings. Because, according to the research, it's ladies first or, as biologists have dubbed it, female proceptivity.

However, women can't simply walk up to a man, slap him on the back, and offer to buy him a drink. Studies show that women who are seen as taking the initiative with men are perceived negatively. This seems to be a paradox. Remember, though, the mating dance is not a simple, straightforward matter of ask and answer. It's all about subtle (usually nonverbal) signals and cues.

Let's start with a fairly simple demonstration of this principle at work. Many women have at one time or another found themselves attracted to a man but uncertain about how to get him to approach her. The answer is quite simple: eye contact, especially combined with a smile. Okay, you say, but how much eye contact? Again, the answer is simple: a lot—probably far more than most women are comfortable with! In a 1985 study, researchers set up a simple test. They had an attractive woman target a man roughly ten feet away and then see what it took to get him to approach her within ten minutes. They tried several variations: eye contact once or several times and either alone or paired with a smile. For women who have been raised under the myth that men are supposed to make the first move, I have some shocking news: men don't just need encouragement. They need *a lot* of encouragement. Multiple times and in multiple ways. Even making eye contact multiple times if that signal wasn't accompanied by a smile had a modest success rate of less than 20 percent. To be highly successful, a woman needed to make eye contact multiple times and accompany that eye contact with a smile. When she did, 60 percent of the men eventually approached her and struck up a conversation.

But that is only one weapon in the female arsenal. Beyond eye contact and smiling, what else can women do? Psychologist Monica Moore has spent thousands of hours watching women flirt with men and has cataloged fifty-two nonverbal signals that women use to draw men's attention. Forthwith, a brief sample of her findings: primping, smiling, nodding, leaning forward, the lip lick, the hair flip, and the object caress. There is also the glance (darting or fixated). The giggle, the skirt hike, and the breast caress. The solitary dance. All the way up to more elaborate techniques, such as the presentation of the neck (a sign of submission in the animal kingdom) and the parade, which is probably self-explanatory. She even ranked them based on how they were used. "Smile at him broadly" was far and away the winner with "throw him a short, darting glance" and "dance alone to the music" tied for a distant second. For those who want the full arsenal, I recommend her article "Nonverbal Courtship Patterns in Women," which appeared in the July 1985 issue of *Ethology and Sociobiology*. For those women who worry that they are not attractive enough to be successful in these circumstances, there is more good news. The number of signals you send counts for far more than how you look. According to Moore, the women who were approached the most often were not those who were the most attractive but those who signaled most frequently— women who sent out more than thirty-five signals an hour averaged more than four approaches an hour. There is no question that thirty-five times an hour is a lot of signal sending, particularly for the shy among us, but (in what is becoming a familiar refrain) *Decoding Love* has never promised that the mating dance was easy.

fact is that most men are more oblivious to nonverbal signals than women are, which isn't to say that they don't respond to them or even that they don't send them. But they do have less conscious awareness of both signals sent and received. Because of men's obtuseness, even signals of rejection have to be stronger for them since they tend to discount those signals more than a woman would.

If you look at how men and women consciously describe the art of seduction, you can quickly see just how oblivious many men are. In one study by biologist Timothy Perper, men and women were asked to write an essay describing how they would seduce someone. Women proved to be virtual Cleopatras in the art of seduction and had detailed strategies for how to seduce a man. They ranged from suggesting returning to "my place," complimenting the man physically, offering to give a back rub, putting on soft music, subtly touching, and so on. Men, on the other hand, were maddeningly vague on the subject. One wrote, "I probably would just try to give the impression that if she wants to have sex, then it's all right with me," an answer that not only explicitly leaves the burden on the woman but doesn't even state what he would do to give the impression that he wanted to have sex. Another wrote, "I would more than likely try in some way to seduce this person." Talk about an answer that begs the question. As one wrote in what could serve as a description for most men, "Seduction is a vague concept for me." Reading these answers, it seems possible that the species itself might cease to exist if women did not step into the breach—which they are far more willing to do than cultural myths suggest. According to Perper, more than

87 percent of the women said that they would be willing to initiate the encounter. And in my own interviews, most women admitted that they were often the ones to get things started.

However, when it comes to the actual sex, women are the ones who become vague in their answers, while men become much more explicit, discussing everything from sucking earlobes to caressing body parts. What this suggests is that men take control when the seduction turns physical, while women play the key role in the early stages. Perper calls it a "division of romantic effort."

After doing the research for this chapter, I now realize that my own lack of awareness about signals bordered on imbecility. I still remember the first time I kissed a girl. Despite ample signaling from her, I stood on her doorway desperately making conversation in the vain hope that my next move would magically materialize. Luckily, she finally put us both out of our misery by asking me if I would like to kiss her. By putting it as a question, I suppose she was successfully skirting the prohibition against being too direct. That pretty much set the tone for most of the rest of my romantic career so that I now find myself wondering how I ever went out with anyone at all. My interviews with men showed that this was not an uncommon reaction. After I described some of the research for this chapter, many of the men wanted lessons in how to get better at deciphering nonverbal communication.

SHALL WE DANCE?

Although I've jokingly used the term mating dance, it is entirely appropriate. The barroom encounter between men and women is choreographed as closely as any ballroom dance. So, let us examine the pas de deux. A number of researchers—people like David Givens and Timothy Perper—have spent inordinate amounts of time in bars mapping all of this out so that we don't have to. They have reduced the mating dance to a science—or, at least, a well-choreographed dance with precise steps that must occur for courtship success. According to Perper in his excellent book *Sex Signals*, there are five stages:

1. Approach;
2. Talk;
3. Turn—what Perper is referring to is how a couple will gradually turn so that their bodies are facing each other;
4. Touch—usually initiated by the woman, so, yes, ladies, you are still in charge;
5. Synchronize—this refers to our tendency to mirror each other's physical movements when we are feeling a connection (recent studies have shown that this can take a number of forms beyond physical mirroring, including voice cadence and length of eye contact).

(Givens has also broken down courtship into five basic phases that are broader but still roughly analogous to Perper: attracting attention, recognition, conversation, touching, and making love.)

This sequence can take anywhere from a few minutes to hours, but there are certain rules the encounter must follow if it is to progress, according to Perper. Each stage is what he calls an escalation point, and each person's response to each escalation is crucial to the outcome. If one person touches the other, but the other never reciprocates, that will derail the encounter, and it will stop escalating. Also, the signals that the two people send to each other must go from less intense to more intense for the couple to move through the five stages. A quick example will show why. If a man expresses strong admiration of the woman in conversation by saying something like, "You are very beautiful" (a strong signal), but she responds tepidly ("Hmmm, well, it's very dark in here"), the man will adjust his enthusiasm level to her own, and the encounter will begin to de-escalate. Perper also found that women are usually the ones to escalate.

Before you run off to the nearest bar and try this out, I do have one warning: all of this usually occurs subconsciously. Attempting to manipulate the process runs a very high risk. If the other person catches you doing it, you can kiss your chances good-bye. So, how should you go about mirroring someone? Studies show that it is best to do it imperfectly and to allow a time lag of a few seconds before you do mirror a movement. My own advice would be to let the mating dance take its natural course and simply use these "rules" as a way to judge whether you and your partner are both feeling the same way about each other.

One final thought for those men and women who are desperate to meet someone when they hit the bars: stay until the end. A group of researchers went to a college bar and asked a number of individuals to rate the attractiveness of the opposite sex at the bar that night. They repeated this three times: at 9 p.m., 10:30 p.m., and midnight. What they found was that both men and women raised their ratings as the time grew later. This effect was even more pronounced for men than for women. Although tempting to dismiss this as a classic case of beer goggles, the researchers determined that the rating's boost was not related to alcohol consumption, which means the goggles were entirely self-induced. So, if you can wait until last call, you just might get lucky.

A FEW MORE UNKIND WORDS FOR SEX

Which brings us once again to sex. Not to beat a dead horse, but I am going to repeat my advice to women: be very careful about whom you sleep with and how quickly you sleep with him. It's clear from a number of studies that some women use sex as one way to lure a man into a long-term relationship, but that is, at best, a risky strategy. In all likelihood, women will fall prey to what some researchers have dubbed an "affective shift." According to one study, men's and women's feelings about their partners change after the first sexual encounter, and the results should give pause to any woman interested in a long-term relationship. For women, there is a distinctly positive shift after first-time sex. In other words, they care more about a man after they have slept with him. There are obvious evolutionary reasons for this: women need to be concerned about finding someone to help raise the children, so they are biologically designed to try to push relationships in the direction of a long-term commitment. This is yet another reason women need to be careful about choosing their sexual partners. Although a woman may think she just wants a fling, she could wake up the next morning and find that she has developed a much stronger attachment to the man than she expected.

Men react in an entirely different fashion to that first encounter—or at least some men do. For a man who has a lot of sexual partners, having sex for the first time with a women leads to a decrease in his physical and sexual attraction for the woman. Again, this makes evolutionary sense. Having successfully seduced the woman, he can now look for a new partner to seduce to increase his chances of genetic success. On the other hand, men who have not slept with a lot of women do not show the same decrease in sexual attraction. This also makes a certain amount of sense. Not having as much success with seduction, these men maximize their chances of genetic success by willingly investing their energy in one woman. Women do not exhibit the same split. Those who have had numerous sexual partners reacted in the same way to a first-time sexual encounter as those who have had only a few, revealing a woman's consistent bias for a long-term relationship. So, women who use sex to try to lure men into a long-term relationship are likely to find themselves getting less than they hoped for and giving more than they anticipated.

HOW DO I LOVE THEE?

Of course, that is only helpful once you know whom you are trying to attract. Can science take us a step closer to cracking the romantic code and identify not just how we should pursue someone but whom we should pursue? The answer is a very limited yes, and the surprising twist is that although much of this book has emphasized how different men and women are, the two sexes are surprisingly similar when it comes to what both are looking for in a long-term relationship. This is not as shocking as it may at first sound. Much of the conflict between men and women arises because of differences in short-term and long-term strategies. When it comes to your marital partner, though, the qualities that make a good husband are not all that different from the qualities that make a good wife.

What is it that we are looking for in a person beyond their physical appearance? We all want a person who loves us, is dependable, and has a pleasant disposition. Of course, what men and women look for is hardly set in stone. According to a 2001 article in the *Journal of Marriage and Family* comparing studies from the 1930s to the 1990s, there has been both change and constancy. Mutual love and attraction have become more important for both men and women, testifying to the increasing dominance of the romantic story line. Men care much less about domestic skills than they once did. And good financial prospects have become increasingly important. Overall, though, there has been a convergence in the qualities that men and women want in a partner.

So just what sort of partner should you be looking for? A dazzling array of tests and profiles have been developed to parse personalities and answer this question. As I discussed earlier, many of these tests have already been pressed into service in one form or another to try to help Internet dating services predict with some degree of accuracy which people might be suitable for one another. We are going to ignore all the complicated ins and outs of those theories for a simple reason that involves some good news and some bad news. First, the bad news. No formula has yet been able to crack the mystery of why two people end up together. That is exactly what most of us would predict, even though dating services like to make extravagant claims to the contrary. Now, for the good news. If you give up on coming up with some perfect

ding "the one," understanding what sort of person-
attractive to you is fairly simple and straightfor-
you a few helpful ideas that, if they won't pinpoint
perfect match, will at least point you in the right direction.

As I said, we are all looking for the same things, which can be
boiled down to three areas. An infinite number of variations of
these three exist, and the importance any one person gives to
each of them will vary. When it comes to a long-term partner,
though, these three categories are the foundation. They are:

1. warmth/loyalty;
2. vitality/attractiveness;
3. status/resources.

That is a wide swath of possibilities, but there is one way we
can narrow down those three. Studies have found a strong correlation between your self-perception and your ideal for a mate.
If you think of yourself as someone who prizes loyalty above all
else, you will want to look for someone who has that same quality. Or if you feel that sensitivity is essential, you should look for
someone who shares that feeling—actually, according to a recent study, we want someone who is slightly better than we are,
so you will probably want someone even more loyal or sensitive
than you are. This is especially true for women who are, to repeat
myself, the choosier sex. The first step in finding a partner, then,
is to identify what qualities about yourself you most value.

Unsurprisingly, both sexes also share similar feelings about what
qualities are the most important. In one 1990 study, both men
and women considered warmth and consideration the most im-

portant qualities. When it comes to intelligence, both sexes want at least average intelligence in someone they are dating, although if the question is whether or not to have sex with someone, men are willing to sleep with someone of less than average intelligence, while women seek someone of more than average intelligence. Women do place a greater emphasis on sincerity, which David Buss argues is a code word to judge a man's commitment. Women also place more emphasis on having a sense of humor.

LEAVE THEM LAUGHING

Humor deserves its own special treatment. As anyone who skims through the personal ads knows, sense of humor is an absolutely essential quality. Everyone wants it in his or her partner, and no one will admit to lacking it. Any time I asked men or women what qualities they looked for, sense of humor was at or near the top of the list. Why should that be the case? Researchers did a very interesting study that helps provide some answers. They asked a group of women to read vignettes about various men. The key variable that changed from story to story was the man's sense of humor. In some stories, the fictional man had an excellent sense of humor. In others, he had an average one. And in still others, he had a poor sense of humor. The study found that men with an excellent sense of humor were endowed by female readers with all sorts of other good qualities. Women saw them as more sensitive, more adaptable, happier, more intelligent, more masculine, and even taller. All of these additional attributes were not because of anything in the vignette. They were entirely the result of the man's sense of humor. In other words, women unconsciously use sense of humor as a proxy for many other traits, such as creativity and intelligence. This helps explain why humor is always high on the list of desired qualities. It is not just for that quality in and of itself but because it acts as a signal for so many other sought-after qualities as well.

To see how deeply this is woven into our psyches, you only need to look at the results when the researchers took into account a woman's fertility. When a woman was at her peak fertility and looking for a short-term relationship, her attraction to the man with an excellent sense of humor spiked sharply. Men with average or below-average humor found their ratings unchanged, which confirms that humor acts as a proxy for good genes in general. Humor may even be worth the importance that so many of us place on it. One study revealed that women's humor rating of their partners significantly predicted their general relationship satisfaction. But there remains a crucial difference between the sexes. Studies show that men tend to be the ones who make the jokes, and women tend to be the ones who laugh at them.

Unfortunately, none of this is the holy grail of dating. At best, it gets you only a small way toward figuring out what to look for in a partner. When it comes to personality, science still only has a rudimentary understanding of why one person is attracted to another.

THE BRAIN—ADDICTED TO LOVE

Many of you clever readers probably have a nagging question in the back of your minds going all the way back to those provocative lap dancers at the start of the chapter. All well and good to give us this advice about things to look for and how to attract a mate, you're thinking, but it sounds as if none of this might be in our control. After all, if attraction is tied to things like a woman's fertility cycle, who cares who is batting whose eyes at whom? And you would be quite right to raise that objection. While it doesn't negate the previous pages, it does leave one area unexplored, and that area may be the most powerful of all: our own body chemistry, those signals ranging from smell to ovulation to hormones over which we have no control.

There is a great deal of emerging scientific evidence that being in love does strange things to the brain. According to functional MRI scans, infatuated love activates the same brain circuits as obsession, mania, and intoxication. One study found that the areas of the brain activated by cocaine were the same ones that became active when lovers were shown photographs of their partners. People in love also have high levels of PEA, a natural amphetamine found in chocolate. It may be what helps fuel the sudden ability to go without sleep as you stay up all night with your lover. Louann Brizendine, a neuropsychiatrist, has compared the brain activity of a person in love to that of a drug addict craving his next fix. And when people talk about the pain of a broken heart, they are being more literal than you would think. Rejection activates the same brain circuits as physical pain. In fact, being in love literally rewires the brain. One of the chemicals released is oxytocin. Along with causing feelings of euphoria, it also appears to melt old neural connections so that large-scale changes in the brain can take place. This makes it easier to learn new things, such as replacing feelings of love for an old partner with feelings of love for a new partner.

These physical manifestations of what once seemed to be merely metaphoric descriptions are not surprising when you start to explore how much *physical* space our sexual organs monopolize in our brains. Stefan Klein writes, "If the size of individual organs were commensurate with the space given them in the brain, the penis and the vagina could easily outweigh the entire upper body." In fact, it's not much of a stretch to say that the brain itself is the most important sexual organ in the body and that, as Helen Fisher claims, the search for love is a fundamental drive like hunger or thirst.

When we fall in love or even when we simply experience desire, a whole slew of chemicals is involved—dopamine, norepinephrine, phenylethylamine, oxytocin, and vasopressin to name just a few. Of course, what goes on in men's brains and what goes on in women's brains are quite dissimilar. For instance, women in love have activity in different regions of their brain than men in love. This difference can be seen in a wide number of related areas as well. Take, for example, the issue of women's sexuality. It is a much more elusive phenomenon than men's sexuality. Physical cues, such as wetness or swelling, do not necessarily indicate sexual arousal or appetite, and according to one study, while heterosexual men were predictably turned on by footage of naked women, the opposite was not true. Videos of naked men did not necessarily cause more arousal for women than the control footage of snowcapped mountains. What really got women going was the degree of sensuality. When that was present, women put men to shame in the polymorphous nature of their desires. Not only did they respond to videos of naked men—they also responded to videos of naked women. In another study, women were even genitally aroused by footage of bonobo chimps mating (which evoked no response from men), although the women did not consciously experience any sense of arousal.

Studies of our neurochemistry can tell us a great deal about the nature of sexual attraction. For example, the waning of desire is a common problem for all couples—and not just the human ones. Researchers have dubbed this the Coolidge effect because of a famous incident involving the former president and his first lady. According to the story, the first couple were separately touring a government farm. Mrs. Coolidge noticed a rooster mounting a hen and asked how often the rooster copulated. The answer was dozens of times a day, to which she replied, "Please tell that to the president." When Coolidge was later told about this exchange, he asked if the rooster always mated with the same hen and was informed that the rooster copulated with different hens. Coolidge smiled pleasantly and said, "Tell that to Mrs. Coolidge."

Scientists can now offer concrete evidence of the Coolidge effect by monitoring the level of dopamine in animals before and after copulation (dopamine has been dubbed the "molecule of desire" because it is the chemical that motivates us to attain our goals). Take a recent study of rats. When a male rat was shown a new female, his dopamine rose 44 percent, a number that continued to increase before sex but that dropped off drastically after the rat climaxed. The second time he copulated with the same female, the spike in dopamine was smaller, and after several times, the dopamine level hardly rose above normal. If you placed a new female rat on display, though, the male rat's dopamine rose by 34 percent. In our age of casual sex, all of this has major implications for our relationships, and a strong chemical argument could be made that people looking for long-term partners would be best served by prolonging the period of courtship. Unfortunately, for the swingers among us, it appears that our grandparents' advice about people not wanting to buy cows when they can get the milk for free has a scientific basis.

Our brains have a funny quirk built into them that enhances this effect. They thrive on a challenge as long as that challenge is not so difficult that it seems impossible. It is the expectation of a reward, rather than the reward itself, that appears to stimulate dopamine production. We all have experienced this at one time or another. Just think back to the last time you deeply longed for something and how achieving that goal proved far less exciting than thinking about it. In fact, even meaningless goals, such as reaching a new level on a video game, can activate our neurons and get our hearts pumping faster. What this means for women is that their best strategy for ratcheting up a man's level of dopamine and making herself more irresistible is to make sex with her a challenging goal. Once sex occurs, a man's dopamine level and his desire will inevitably fall off, although a woman can probably maintain it at a higher level if sex does not become a foregone conclusion but something that a man has to earn on a continual basis.

THE SCENT OF ATTRACTION

Of course, once scientists started to consider the chemical basis for love, they realized that what frequently underlies attraction is not strangers in the night exchanging glances but exchanging smells. For a long time, scientists dismissed as preposterous the whole idea that humans could be attracted to one another based on smell. In recent years, though, they have discovered that smell can and often does play a crucial role, which brings me to one of my favorite experiments—the smelly T-shirt test.

It could have been worse. Scientists could have asked us to smell one another's urine. The first inklings that smell might play a role in human attraction came not from humans but from rats, specifically from a segment of DNA called the major histocompatibility complex or MHC for short, a sequence of more than fifty genes located along a single chromosome that is different for each and every individual. The reason behind this almost infinite diversity is that the MHC acts as a kind of warning system for the body by detecting disease and alerting the body's defenses to attack, and it has to deal with a bewildering multitude of attackers.

One of the unusual aspects of the MHC is that it is codominant, rather than dominant. With a trait controlled by a dominant gene such as eye color, only the version from one parent will be expressed. With codominant genes, though, both versions continue to function in the offspring. This is a great advantage when it comes to fighting disease. If a father's genes contain immunity to one variant of the disease, while a mother's genes contain immunity to a different variant of the same disease, the offspring will have immunity to both versions of the disease.

Now, back to those pesky rats. It turns out that when a female mouse was offered two different males with which to mate, she always chose the one whose MHC genes were most different from her own. This makes sense as that choice will increase the immunity of her offspring. Her method of selection? Smelling the urine of the male rats. This put sex researchers off the scent, as it were, because humans do not typically make a habit of smelling one another's urine. But then researchers stumbled on a very interesting discovery—humans can smell the difference among mice that differ only in their MHC without having to rely on urine at all. With that, a Swiss biologist named Claus Wedekind designed an experiment to see if he could discover a similar ability in women smelling the MHC of men (women have greater smell sensitivity than men), and thus, the great smelly T-shirt experiment was born. Although Wedekind's findings are better known than most of the studies I discuss, they still deserve close attention because the key element driving smell preference is often not explained, and the shocking results relating to contraception are frequently left out.

More than eighty college students participated in the study. The men were given cotton T-shirts to sleep in for two consecutive nights. To guard against any wayward smells creeping into the picture, they were told not to eat spicy foods, not to smoke, and not to drink any liquor. They also had to avoid any deodorants, cologne, or perfumed soaps. And, of course, no sex. During the day, their T-shirts were kept in a sealed plastic container.

The women were also primed for the experiment. For two weeks prior to the test, they used a nasal spray to protect the mucous membranes lining their nose. Around the time they were ovulating, when their smell was enhanced, they were put to the test: a row of boxes with a hole cut in the top, each containing the T-shirt of one of the men. After inhaling deeply from each box, the women rated each man's shirt for sexiness, pleasantness, and intensity of smell. What the researchers discovered demolished any lingering doubts about the role of smell in attraction.

Wedekind and his staff found that how a woman rated a man's smell depended entirely upon how much of their MHC profiles overlapped. Because a person's MHC profile is incredibly idiosyncratic, what smells good to one woman will not necessarily smell good to another, and short of genetic testing, there is no easy way to predict what a woman will find appealing. For instance, race does not exert much influence on it. All of this made the results of the study even more astounding. The more a man's MHC profile differed, the more the woman rated his smell as pleasant and sexy (a later study found that you can be too different—if there are no MHC genes in common, women are not attracted to the man's smell).

The evidence also suggested that this attraction was not confined to the lab. Women said that the smells they preferred reminded them of current or ex-boyfriends roughly twice as often as men with similar MHC profiles, so smell had likely played an important role in their real world mate selection as well. No matter what the MHC profile, though, strong body odor was a turn-off. Researchers theorized that a strong body odor is often an indicator of disease, so that women may have evolved an aversion to strong smells as a means of avoiding a genetically unfit mate. In fact, odor appears to be yet another marker of genetic fitness. In a different study, women judged symmetrical men to be better smelling than their nonsymmetrical counterparts.

There was one other surprising finding: women taking oral contraceptives had preferences that were the opposite of women not on the pill. They chose men who had similar MHC profiles. To give you some idea of how potentially disturbing this reversal is, women generally described the smell from men with similar

MHC profiles as reminding them of their father's or brother's odor. Traditionally, it may have made sense for a woman to stay close to her family during her pregnancy to ensure her protection and care. But that evolutionary development is clearly being blindsided by scientifically engineered contraceptives, which fool a woman's body into thinking that it is pregnant. As if that wasn't bad enough, another study has shown that women on the pill see the world in a more platonic light, which is clearly counterproductive for single women looking to find a partner because it might blind them to the romantic possibilities around them.

Similar MHC genes have also been shown to cause a host of problems for couples. According to one study, partners who have more difficulty conceiving a child share significantly more of their MHC genes than couples who have dissimilar MHCs. Doctors have also found that couples with more similar MHC profiles suffer from higher rates of miscarriage. It even has an effect on sexual fidelity. As MHC profiles become more similar, researchers have found that a woman's sexual responsiveness to her partner diminishes. She is more attracted to other men, and she is, on average, unfaithful with a greater number of men. With 50 percent of the profile in common, a woman has a 50 percent chance of sleeping with another man. These studies clearly suggest that any woman who is serious about finding a long-term partner should avoid oral contraceptives. By outwitting nature, we may have actually outwitted ourselves and undermined an important element of mate selection—smell.

If a woman does decide to go off the pill, I do have to warn that there will be one unexpected downside if she chooses to use condoms instead—she will no longer have the medicinal benefits of semen. That may sound even more preposterous than the T-shirt study, but it's the truth. Unlikely as it sounds, semen contains powerful, mood-enhancing chemicals that are absorbed through the vaginal wall (digestion is a different matter, so this doesn't apply to fellatio). According to a recent study, women who don't use condoms and have regular sex are less depressed than women who use condoms or women who aren't having sex.

Of course, women have probably intuitively understood the power of smell all along. A surprising number of women I interviewed said that smell played a crucial role in their dating, and some even claimed that they could immediately "smell" if a man was right for them. One woman even said that she liked to smell her boyfriend's armpit—and not when he was fresh out of the shower. Not since Walt Whitman have I seen such a ringing endorsement of the sweet smell of armpits. Our hygiene-obsessed society makes it more difficult for women to smell whether a protective partner has the right stuff or not, which might help explain why kissing plays such a large role in most relationships. Our saliva also contains traces of our MHC, so kissing can reveal what our daily showering hides. You do have to exercise some caution when relying on your nose, though. Fragrances can fool even the most astute sniffer, so you need to make sure that you are smelling the unadulterated scent.

FICKLENESS, THY NAME IS FERTILITY CYCLE

It is possible that the chemistry of the body, particularly hormones, also offers an explanation for the fickleness attributed to women. For example, a woman's ovulation cycle can have a dramatic effect on what sort of man she finds attractive. Studies have shown that during ovulation women find masculine faces more attractive but find feminine faces more attractive the rest of the time (other traits such as voice follow a similar pattern). Women during ovulation also show a greater preference for the smell of symmetrical men. Masculine faces and symmetricality are signs of health, so there are very good evolutionary reasons why women would have developed an unconscious preference for these markers of genetic superiority. Intriguingly, women do not show a preference for the smell of symmetrical men when they are not ovulating. This may be due to the unconscious realization that men with the best genes often don't make the most faithful partners, which suggests just how subtle our evolutionary tendencies can be. Even the smell of other women can influence female behavior. In one study, women exposed to the smell of other women who were breast-feeding found that their sexual desire spiked 17–24 percent. Truly bold women can try to pull off a daring stunt with their copulins, which are fatty acids found in vaginal secretions. In one study, while men did not rate the smell of copulins as pleasant, they had a dramatic effect on how the men viewed women. After being exposed to the smell, the men gave higher ratings for attractiveness to photos of women, and their testosterone levels spiked. The less attractive the woman, the more her rating went up. If men want to pull off a similar feat, they can try to plant some sweat under a woman's nose. In one study, women rated men's faces and then were exposed to a small amount of underarm sweat and asked to rate the faces again. After smelling the sweat, the women raised their ratings substantially.

It's not simply how we judge looks that can be affected by things like smell and ovulation—these things can also alter what sort of personality a woman finds attractive. In a study run by Geoffrey Miller and Martie Haselton, women read stories that described either a creative, poor man or an uncreative, rich man. When women were near their peak fertility, they preferred creativity to wealth for a short-term relationship, offering evidence that ovulation can dramatically affect a woman's mate choice by pushing her to choose good genes over a good dad, particularly when she is not making a long-term decision. Marriage itself influences a woman's preferences. In another examination of the influence of smell on female choice, a woman with a partner preferred the smell of more dominant men, while single women showed no preference. Researchers have suggested that single women were interested in securing a partner, but once that was taken care of, women turned to the pursuit of the best genes. Ovulation may even provide an explanation for the female complaint that all the good men are taken. According to a 2008 study, women with partners found men in a relationship more attractive during periods of low fertility, but they preferred single men (if they displayed masculine traits) during periods of high fertility. Again, this shift in preference seems to correspond to a good genes/good dad split, with ovulation increasing a woman's attraction to single, masculine men for their genes but with low fertility shifting their attraction to men who show an ability to commit to a long-term relationship (i.e., a man already in a relationship). So, the next time a woman finds herself lamenting the lack of available men, she can perhaps blame it on her fertility cycle.

MEN GET MOODY, TOO

Don't worry, ladies. A man is ruled just as much by his own body chemistry, although it does not function in the same way that a woman's does. Let's return to that odiferous object of scientific inquiry, the sweaty T-shirt. Researchers decided to run a similar smell test on men. They gave women cotton T-shirts to wear during different phases of their menstrual cycle and then had men smell the results. What men honed in on was not a woman's MHC profile but her ovulation cycle. Rating T-shirts for pleasantness and sexiness, men gave women who were ovulating or about to ovulate a much higher rating than women who were approaching menstruation. According to another study, women reported that their partners became more loving and attentive during their ovulations as well as more jealous of other men. In other words, men aren't particularly focused on finding a woman with a different immune profile, but they have an uncanny ability to seek out women who are at their peak fertility. This seems to hold true in the real world as well as the experimental one. In one barroom study, men initiated touching with ovulating women more than nonovulating women. This all makes evolutionary sense. In general, men want to have sex with as many fertile women as possible, regardless of whether or not the woman is a good genetic fit. For women, though, each pregnancy represents a huge investment, so it makes sense that they would devote a lot more (unwitting) attention to ensure that the baby has the best genetic chance of success.

Men also have their own hormonal fluctuations to worry about. Their testosterone goes through a series of peaks and valleys throughout the day, but it can still serve as an indicator for more significant traits, such as mood and aggression. Some men are naturally low in testosterone, which is good for society because if all men were alpha males, the fighting would never stop. We would constantly find ourselves locked in Travis Bickle–like arguments. "Are you looking at me?" "No, but are *you* looking at *me*?" Important life changes can also influence a man's testosterone. When men are in a stable relationship, their baseline level of testosterone drops. For example, married men have lower testosterone on average than single men, and married men with children have less testosterone on average than married men without children. But their testosterone will ratchet back up if the relationship becomes unstable. A high-testosterone man will also behave more aggressively when it comes to dating. A study was done in which different men competed for the attention of a woman. Men with high testosterone would make fun of the other man, criticize him, and refuse to laugh at his jokes. Women interested in a long-term relationship should try to avoid men who display the traits of someone with high testosterone—they tend to marry less frequently, have more affairs, abuse their wives more, and divorce more often.

STARRY-EYED OEDIPUS

In a result that will delight Freudians, it appears that although men may not want to sleep with their mothers, they do prefer women who remind them of their mothers—at least that's what the evidence from the animal kingdom seems to suggest. In one study, the mothers of infant male rats were doused with lemon scent. Later, the males were paired with some female rats with lemon scent and some without it. It was no contest. The males mounted the lemon-scented rats sooner and ejaculated more quickly. One man I interviewed admitted that he had a serious relationship with a woman and found himself attracted to her perfume, only to realize later the rather distressing news that the perfume was the same one his mother used.

Luckily, we seem to have evolved mechanisms to protect us against our own personal Oedipal drama. One researcher decided to take a look at marriage on an Israeli kibbutz. Because of the way the kibbutzim is structured, girls and boys are raised in close proximity, almost like brothers and sisters of the same family. When researchers looked at their marriage patterns, it turned out that even though they would not have violated any incest taboos, children of the kibbutzim almost never married. Of the 2,769 marriages, only thirteen were between children who grew up together, and even in those cases, at least one of the children moved in after the age of six. So, it appears that the ultimate antiaphrodisiac is growing up from a young age in close proximity to one another.

Of course, if you want to maximize the number of children you have, there is a powerful incentive to choose someone in your extended family: greater fecundity. According to a study of the Icelandic population, the ideal degree of relatedness to produce the maximum number of children and grandchildren is a union between cousins of the third or fourth degree. Any closer and the couple risks inbreeding. Any further and the couple risks running into genetic incompatibility problems. Who knew that extended family reunions are a potential dating scene?

YOUR CHEATING . . . GENE

It also appears that there may be a genetic component that determines how likely a man is to cheat, what some researchers have dubbed the "promiscuity gene." They have found that there is a variant in some genes for the D4 receptor, a dopamine receptor. Because dopamine is the chemical that stimulates us to want things and underlies everything from sexual attraction to gambling addiction, a change in dopamine reception can have a major influence on our behavior. Men with the promiscuity version of the D4 receptor have an increased desire for erotic adventure and have 20 percent more sexual partners than the average man. Researchers estimate that roughly 30 percent of men carry this gene, but before women go on a genetic witch hunt to weed out these philandering miscreants, they should know that, while similar research has not been done on women, it is very likely that some women have a similar genetic variation. Remember— all those children who are not the product of their legal parents' loins need both a cheating father and a cheating mother.

For a more precise take on a man's ability—or inability, if you are a glass-half-empty kind of gal—to be faithful, we need to take a look at the rather unprepossessing and very monogamous prairie vole. Upon reaching maturity, the male latches onto virtually the first available female partner. The couple will spend an entire day copulating like, well, voles and then spend the rest of their lives together. Even separation does not change the bond, and when one of the partners dies, the other vole, in a remarkable display of fidelity, does not take a new mate. However, there is another type of mole—the montane vole—which is polygamous.

So, what accounts for the unstinting and admirable monogamy of the prairie vole and the promiscuous polygamy of his montane cousin? It probably all comes down to one small slice of DNA that acts as a blueprint for a particular type of vasopressin receptor in the brain, and the reason that receptor is so important is that the hormone vasopressin, which is released during sex, plays a central role for males in forming monogamous bonds. The prairie voles have this slice of genetic code, which means that they have a lot more vasopressin receptors in their brain than the montane voles. That makes them much more susceptible to the pair-bonding power of vasopressin. When scientists inserted this genetic code into montane voles, they immediately became as monogamous as the prairie voles.

Vasopressin is so powerful that prairie voles don't even need the sex to form a monogamous bond. They just need the vasopressin. If injected with it, they form a lifelong bond with the first available female, even though they have not had sex. When the vasopressin is blocked, the male vole acts as if he has never seen the female before, even after having repeated sex with her. How many women know that feeling? Vasopressin (and oxytocin for the females) has even been used to create monogamy among polygamous house mice. In a final twist, it turns out that all voles are not created equal when it comes to vasopressin. Further study revealed that some males have a longer version of the gene than others and that those with the longest versions are also the most reliable partners.

So, what sort of vasopressin receptors are men equipped with? The answer is far more complicated than anyone first imagined. Researchers have already found that the human version of the gene comes in at least *seventeen* different lengths, a number that is likely to grow as more work is done (similar work also needs to be done for women and oxytocin). What this means is that there is a wide spectrum of possibilities when it comes to the issue of how genetically predisposed individual men may be toward monogamy. Still, it may hold the key to understanding long-term bonds between men and women. To give you some idea of how significant this particular gene might be to male behavior, a shorter version of the gene has been found in those with autism, a condition characterized by difficulty forming relationships with other people. As men realize the possible seductive power of their receptivity to vasopressin, we may one day find that they have stopped bragging about the size of their members in order to brag about the size of their vasopressin receptors, which would, I think, have to be considered at least a small step forward.

Of course, any definitive answers to the chemical nature of love are still a distant hope, but scientists are making progress. As we have seen, researchers have been able to sniff out at least a few clues about the elusive nature of attraction between a man and a woman. If all else fails in your search for love, remember that you can always simply follow your nose.

A Second Brief Intermission to Focus—Finally—On the More Traditional Subject of a Book About Attraction: Practical Advice

THE REAL QUESTION IS, CAN SCIENCE PROVIDE PRACTI-cal advice for all of us wayward daters? The surprising answer is yes. Some of that advice is common sense, and some of it is unexpected. Before I go into any of it, though, I want to issue a warning. I have read far more dating books than any human being should, and they have convinced me of one thing: be leery of anyone who confidently offers surefire dating tips. Most of these books are based on little more than a mishmash of anecdotes. I can promise that the information in this section is based on the same scientific studies and surveys as the rest of the book. That said, please treat what you are about to read as a casual buffet of dating tips from which you can pick and choose as you please.

I've broken this part into three sections:

1. For Him and Her;
2. For Him;
3. For Her.

FOR HIM AND HER

Learn to love yourself. I know that sounds incredibly unscientific and touchy-feely—I can almost hear strains of "Kumbaya" in the background—but a great deal of research backs it up. Simply put, the more you have a positive view of yourself, the more likely you are to fall in love. And the more likely the love will be healthful, rather than destructive.

Although we like to believe we aren't shallow people who simply judge a book by its cover, research shows that first impressions are very important. According to a 1993 study, people viewing a videotape of a teacher were able, after viewing the tape for only thirty seconds, to do a very good job of predicting how a teacher would be evaluated by his or her students. And here's the real kicker: the thirty seconds included only nonverbal interaction and physical attractiveness. If you are unsure how to make a good first impression, there are many books that have been written on the subject, although I have one suggestion: focus on the other person. A good first impression depends more on showing interest in someone than in showing off.

Selective desire is better than generalized desire—in other words, don't hit on every eligible person you meet like some kind of Energizer bunny of flirting. In a recent study, people who were seen as having generalized desire were perceived as less desirable, while people who showed desire for just one person were viewed much more positively. Also, in a study of speed dating, researchers found that the choosier people were, the higher others rated their appeal.

Try to bump into the object of your desire as often as possible. Familiarity has a powerful effect on attractiveness. In one study, men and women were shown a number of photographs and were asked to select the photograph of a person they could imagine marrying. Afterward, some of the photographs were projected several times on a screen, and then the participants were asked to select a photograph again. In a number of cases, both men and women changed their initial selection and switched to one of the photographs that had been projected several times. The other benefit of this for the less attractive among us is that physical attractiveness becomes less important over time as what researchers call the "familiarity effect" takes hold.

Keep your face animated—although not so animated that you come across as crazy. Research shows that a face animated with expression is seen as more attractive than one that is devoid of emotion. This is why people with good poker faces have trouble getting dates.

Use eye contact. We've already discussed this, but I can't emphasize enough how powerful this is. Eye contact can boost attractiveness, regardless of the sex. In a study conducted by psychologist Arthur Aron, total strangers were paired up and had a ninety-minute conversation in which they shared personal details about themselves. Then they gazed silently into each other's eyes for four minutes. Afterward, they were asked about their feelings for the other person, and many of the participants admitted that they felt strongly attracted. How strongly? Some of the couples eventually *married*! Not bad for four minutes of eye contact.

Don't obsess about how you look. Obsess about how you act. A recent study showed that while attractiveness, emotional expressiveness, and social skills all contributed to someone's likability, attractiveness was the least important of the three.

If you aren't attractive, at least try to hang out with attractive people. A study found that people sitting next to attractive people were also judged to be more attractive because of their proximity.

Show the person that you like him or her. Researchers have discovered that how much we think someone likes us has a powerful effect on how much we like them. I realize that it is somewhat disheartening to consider that we have not evolved much beyond junior high school when serious flirting involved passing a note telling someone that you liked them and asking them to check a box if they liked you, but it's true. Studies have found, for example, that a similarity in attitudes has far less of an influence over how much someone likes you than does reciprocity (the feeling that both people like each other). And once both people are convinced that the other person does like them, it can create a positive feedback loop where increasingly positive feelings are created.

In fact, being liked or disliked tends to become a self-fulfilling prophecy because it ends up affecting one's behavior and, thus, shaping others' perception. We act as if we are liked or disliked, and people tend to treat us in ways that fit with our behavior.

Similarity in values still counts, though, so don't neglect that. In one study, blind dates were randomly told that they were similar or dissimilar in their attitudes toward life. Guess which couples ended up liking each other a lot more? The ones who had been told they were similar. Despite the premise behind almost all romantic comedies that opposites attract, dissimilar attitudes tend to repulse possible suitors. According to a 1986 study, people who said nothing were rated significantly more likable by the speakers than people who expressed dissimilar attitudes.

If you do find yourself attracted to someone with dissimilar attitudes, make sure that you laugh at his or her jokes, because humor plays a powerful role in attraction. Researchers led students to believe that an unseen stranger was 90 percent similar or dissimilar. The students read a joke to the stranger over an intercom, and the stranger either laughed or offered a neutral response. The result? Laughter proved far more important than similarity. When the students' attraction to the stranger was later measured, the 90 percent dissimilar person who laughed at the joke was seen as more attractive than the 90 percent similar person who didn't.

Be choosy, but not too choosy. Let me be a little more precise. You should send out signals that you are choosy but not toward the person you are trying to attract. Several studies were unable to find evidence to support the idea that playing hard to get is a successful strategy. While people like choosy partners, studies show that they only like them when they are choosy with others, not with themselves. In one study, men and women were presented with a choice between people who were "very choosy," "choosy," and "not choosy." Both sexes were most attracted to people described as choosy and not attracted to the very choosy, with women even more negative about this category than men.

Try to avoid dating someone out of your league. Studies have shown that dating someone with a similar level of attractiveness leads to greater satisfaction and success in the relationship.

Try to marry someone who has had roughly the same number of prior sexual partners as yourself. Research has found that, on average, these couples feel greater commitment and satisfaction about their relationship and also experience greater love for each other.

Lay off the porn. Studies have shown that men and women who view X-rated materials are less satisfied with their partners and less supportive of marriage.

Obstacles can increase attraction—if they come from *outside* the relationship. Researchers have documented a "Romeo and Juliet effect," finding that both married and unmarried couples exhibited a strong correlation between the love they have for another and the level of parental interference. More interference led to greater love.

Take a date to *Knocked Up*, not *There Will Be Blood*, and by ex-
tension, look for any ways to improve a date's mood. Studies
show that a good mood enhances attraction, while a bad mood
can snuff it out.

Give the person a prolonged hug—provided, of course, that the
hug won't come across as creepy. After a twenty-second hug,
the brain releases oxytocin, which increases feelings of trust.

If you have been chatting with someone for a while and want to
gauge how things are going, try to see if the two of you have developed any synchrony. When you turned to face her, did she turn
to face you? When he leaned forward, did you soon do the same
thing? But don't simply start mirroring the other person—he'll
think you are some weird Marcel Marceau impersonator.

When you are dating someone, treat him or her as if he or she
already has the qualities you seek. Studies have shown that people
try to live up to the good opinion that their partners have of them.

FOR HIM

In the end, none of this is rocket science. The qualities that attract women are rather predictably the qualities that any woman
would want in a long-term partner. According to one study,
women claimed that the best methods for attracting them were
showing good manners and being helpful and caring. Not surprisingly, another study revealed that these were also the quali-

ties about which men often tried to deceive women. Some men admit that they often volunteer to take a friend's puppy for a walk because it sends such powerful signals about the man being a caring individual. You can take this to its logical extreme and ask what effect taking care of a baby might have on women, and researchers have done precisely this. Women were shown pictures of the same man standing alone, interacting positively with a baby, or ignoring a baby in distress. Unsurprisingly, women were most attracted to the man when he was playing with the baby. Alas, the same signal will not work for women—a similar study done with a woman showed no change in the men's opinion of the woman's attractiveness, no matter what she was doing with the baby. Of course, if casual sex is all that is on offer, displays of physical prowess by men greatly increase their chances of success.

Forget the big come-on. You don't need the right line to meet a woman. According to one magazine poll, just saying hello works 71 percent of the time for men (it works 100 percent of the time for women, but we already know that women are the choosier sex).

Are you the type of person who starts jabbing your finger at someone when you get excited? Stop doing or making gestures that could be perceived as threatening. You should treat your physical approach with the care of a bird-watcher trying not to scare away his quarry. According to anthropologist David Givens, an open palm is a good, nonthreatening movement. As for touch, he recommends a hand to the small of her back when assisting her, as a way to convey self-assurance with an undertone of sexuality.

You don't need Hans and Franz to pump you up. Women prefer an average-size male torso and consider a heavily muscular body unattractive.

Although sweatpants *are* comfortable, think about putting on something a little nicer. When women were shown pictures of men, the better dressed the subject was, the higher they were inclined to rank him in all sorts of areas, including the likelihood of having a one-night stand with him.

Lay off the cologne. According to a recent study, the smell of it turns women off. How did the researchers know? The women's vaginal blood flow decreased. Instead, try eating some Good 'n Plenty candy. For some reason, that smell increased vaginal blood flow.

The advice your father gave you on handshakes is absolutely true: the firmer, the better. According to new research, handgrip strength in men is directly related to reproductive fitness. Researchers have found that men with strong grips are healthier and more dominant, have a more masculine body type, have sex at a younger age, and have more sexual encounters. Unfortunately, you can't simply buy handgrips and fake it—grip strength is largely genetic and is tied to your testosterone production.

For the squeakers out there, try to speak with a low-pitched voice. Women prefer a lower-pitched voice and see it as attractive, healthier, and more masculine. It's likely an evolutionary signal of genetic fitness. In a study of hunter-gatherers, men with lower-pitched voices had more children.

Hang out with attractive women. One study found that men were judged to be more attractive when they were with an attractive woman than they were when they were by themselves (the reverse also held true—men with unattractive women were judged to be less attractive).

Become a feminist—not because it's the right thing to do but for the chicks! According to one study, a man's belief in equality between the sexes had the greatest influence on both a woman's platonic and romantic attraction to him.

If you get a woman back to your place, put on rock music, not jazz. One study showed that women who were listening to rock music judged photos of men as significantly more attractive than women who were judging the photos without music or with jazz playing.

Don't be afraid to rent a Bette Midler movie and get in touch with your feminine side. In one study, when women were given a choice between a man who was interested in stereotypically masculine activities versus a man who was interested in masculine and feminine activities, the women viewed the second man as more likable, intelligent, and honest. Another study has shown that dominance in a man only appeals to women if he is also helpful and cooperative.

Although you may rarely leave your couch to do anything more than pay for your takeout, emphasize your ambition and willingness to work hard. Men consistently underestimate how important these qualities are to women.

If you're not tall, consider getting lifts. In personal ads, men who said they were tall received more responses than men who didn't mention their height.

FOR HER

You are not the helpless pawn of love, and men are not the cold-hearted cynics. Studies show that men actually fall in love faster. In addition, researchers have found that women tend to be more pragmatic and realistic when it comes to love.

Before you complain that there are no eligible men in your life, take a second look at your male friends and see if any of them strike your fancy. According to research, men are almost twice as sexually attracted to their female friends as women are to their male friends.

You should take the same attitude toward men as the Missouri state motto: show me! In other words, be skeptical of the promises that men make. It's true that you are much better at picking up signals than men are. You are also far more adept at evaluating facial expressions and do a better job of reading another person's mind. In fact, women are better at a whole range of skills—reading lips, deciphering body language—that should make it far easier for her to decode the signals, sexual or otherwise, that men are sending out. Unfortunately, all of these advantages are a classic Red Queen situation in which men have also improved their ability to deceive women, so that nothing more has been achieved than an uneasy stalemate.

And don't get too cocky about your greater verbal skills because they are also an Achilles' heel. Women are far more likely to pore over conversations with men trying to tease out the nuances of what they said and to have long, detailed conversations with their friends about the man in question. This is not necessarily a good idea, and it also helps explain the success of the book *He's Just Not That Into You*. Instead of attempting painstaking analysis, keep that skeptical attitude, and see if his actions demonstrate the same level of commitment as his words.

You don't need to be a girly girl. Just as women like men who show both masculine and feminine qualities, men like women who show both qualities as well.

If you can't decide whether you need a facial or more time at the gym, hit the gym. Studies show that men care more about a great body than a great face. A woman with an unattractive body gets a lower attractiveness score than a woman with an unattractive face.

Toss out the rice crackers, and treat yourself to a cheeseburger. Despite the inhuman thinness of runway models, studies show that men prefer women who are a normal weight, rather than overly thin, and also that women overestimate how skinny men want them to be. Research also shows that women think hygiene and cleanliness are more important to men than they actually are, so if you are really bold, you can lighten up on your bathing regimen as well.

If you *are* worried about your weight but don't really want to diet, wear a spicy floral perfume fragrance. In one study, women who wore a perfume with that profile were judged on average to be twelve pounds lighter. No other scent had the same effect.

Imitate Rapunzel, and grow your hair long. According to a recent study, men rated the faces of women as prettier when they were surrounded by medium or long hair with the biggest gains for women who were the least attractive. Or you can use your haircut to signal your personality. Men viewed women with longer hair as healthy, intelligent, and mature, while women with short hair were seen as youthful, honest, and caring.

Speak with a high-pitched voice. Men find it more appealing. Well, within reason. You don't need to shatter any crystal glasses.

Wear lipstick. In one study, men's first impression of a woman's attractiveness was much higher when the woman wore lipstick.

You don't have to worry that much about what you wear because men certainly don't. When men were shown pictures of women who were very attractive, moderately attractive, or unattractive, they were always interested in having sex with the moderately and very attractive, regardless of how they were dressed, and no amount of dressing up changed their level of interest in the unattractive women.

Forget all those ridiculously sized breasts staring out at you from men's magazines. Your breasts are probably fine the way they are. Men prefer women with a medium bust, despite what cultural stereotypes suggest.

Feel free to act confused when faced with any sort of complicated machinery like a stapler. According to studies, men want to help women by actively solving problems for them.

It's not a bad idea to downplay your love of Heidegger and play up your fondness for Hello Kitty. Men value intelligence and ambition but only if they do not exceed their own ambition and intelligence. One study of speed dating, for example, revealed that men were much less likely to choose a woman who was more ambitious than they were.

Although you may have a bankroll like a hip-hop mogul, don't flash the Benjamins. Studies show that men prefer to be the main breadwinner and want women who make less money than they do and have a lower-status job.

Don't be afraid to reach out and touch someone. In one study, a volunteer would pretend to be taking a survey and would stop someone. The volunteer would then drop the surveys and see who helped pick them up. The biggest effect? When a woman volunteer touched someone on the upper arm. That single gesture created, by far, the biggest boost in people offering to help pick up the surveys. It even works for women in the workplace. Researchers studied what happened when hand touching occurred in a professional situation. While the effect was ambivalent for men who touched women's hands, the results were uniformly positive for women who touched men's hands.

NOT FOR HIM OR FOR HER

I wouldn't be doing my job if I didn't provide you with a list of turnoffs as well as turn-ons. A dating service called "It's Just Lunch" did a survey of the biggest pet peeves, and they provide a useful overview of things to avoid. Most of them are things that any person with common sense would steer clear of, but the fact that they all appear on this list means that common sense does not play as big a role in guiding behavior as one would hope.

46% listed answering a cell phone call during the meal.

41% said being rude to the waitstaff.

26% of men and 37% of women complained of their lunch partners talking too much about themselves.

30% listed talking about an ex.

45% of men objected to women who talked about their weight or their newest diet.

56% of women complained about men showing more interest in the waitress than in them.

The good news for women is that men remain much less picky, even when it comes to annoying habits. Only 42 percent of women said they would go out on a date with a man who exhibited one of her pet peeves compared to 71 percent of men.

6

The End of Dating

What I Learned About Marriage

I F THERE IS AN UNSPOKEN BIAS TO MY APPROACH, IT IS MY hope that you will find a long-term relationship. That's why I'm ending a book about dating and attraction with a chapter about marriage. It didn't seem right to stop at the altar. Getting happily married is of little use if you can't stay happily married. And it's the *staying* married that is the problem.

I've only been married a few years, so I certainly can't claim any expertise based on personal experience. The funny thing is, though, that even longtime couples don't have a clue what the secret to success is. When I asked them why they had thrived, most laughed and said something along the lines of, "Who knows?" The good news is that researchers have spent a lot of time examining marriages and have come up with some surprising answers about why a marriage does or doesn't work.

WHY YOU SHOULD TIE THE KNOT

For people still on the fence about marriage who think that maybe the healthiest response is simply to avoid the entire institution, there is abundant evidence that you will be better off in the long run as part of a married couple. Most important, you will very likely lead a happier life because of it. In one recent survey, 40 percent of married adults said that they were very satisfied compared to only 25 percent of people who had never been married (a result duplicated in a number of other studies). Single people also suffer from depression at far higher rates. Marriage proved more important as a predictor of happiness than one's job or one's finances or one's community. Why? It turns out that there are all sorts of built-in benefits for married couples.

Let's start with sex. Although the marital bed has long been a source of humor, married couples are having more and better sex than the swinging singles. According to a national survey, 42 percent of married women said that their sex lives were extremely emotionally and physically satisfying compared to 31 percent of single women who had a sexual partner. How important is sex to happiness? If I were going to write the world's shortest self-help book, it would be: more sex! A slew of studies have found connections between healthy sexual activity and longevity. In one study, the death rate for the least sexually active group was twice as high as the most active group. Economists have even quantified the benefits in dollars. As I mentioned in the chapter on economics, increasing the frequency of sexual intercourse from once a month to once a week generates the same amount of happiness as earning an additional $50,000 a year. Economists have also placed a value on marriage itself. A lasting marriage is the equivalent of earning an extra $115,000 annually.

Scientists have discovered all sorts of benefits due to regular sex—better blood flow and circulation, boosting the immune system, warding off colds and infections, making us less susceptible to depression. A survey of 16,000 Americans found that those who had the most sex were also the happiest. What does this have to do with getting married? Married people have a huge built-in advantage when it comes to regular sex for the simple reason that they have a lifelong sexual partner. That's not to say that they don't face their own challenges, such as maintaining passion for one another over the years, but they do have more sex—on average 30 percent more—and better sex, according to the studies.

There are other benefits as well. Even leaving sex aside, marriage improves your health. As we saw in chapter 3½, single people have significantly higher rates of mortality (50 percent higher for women, and a whopping 250 percent higher for men), and not being married reduces the average man's life more than heart disease. Not being married shortens a woman's life more than cancer or living in poverty. There are a host of reasons for this. Men are likely to cut back on a range of unhealthy activities, such as drinking, when they get married. Marriage also brings significant economic advantages. Married men and women enjoy higher average household incomes. In 1997, married couples averaged $47,129 compared to $26,203 for single men and $15,892 for single women.

Perhaps most important, there are the subtle and less quantifiable benefits. What sort of value do you place on companionship? It is difficult to put a number on that, but studies have shown that loneliness causes stress and weakens the immune system. We are social beings, and marriage is the great bulwark against finding ourselves alone. Luckily, most seem to realize this. When people are asked to name their top goals, a happy marriage always heads the list. For those who want more evidence on the benefits of matrimony, I invite you to read Maggie Gallagher and Linda Waite's *The Case For Marriage*, which systematically lays out all of these advantages and numerous others that accrue to happily married couples. But these numbers come with a big caveat—an unhappy marriage can turn these rosy statistics in the other direction. According to one study, an unhappy marriage increases your chances of getting sick by 35 percent and shortens your life by an average of four years. And economists have estimated that getting divorced is the equivalent of losing $66,000 annually.

MARRIAGE AND ITS DISCONTENTS

Of course, if a happy marriage was easy to achieve, we'd have a much lower divorce rate and far fewer affairs. Unfortunately, it's much easier to fall in love than it is to stay in love. Just as we can use the body's own chemistry to chart the effect of infatuation, we can also use it to understand that waning desire is a natural part of any long-term relationship. As Oscar Wilde said, "The essence of romance is uncertainty," but uncertainty is precisely what you are giving up when you get married. Sadly, finding the right person can never be reduced simply to smelling sweaty T-shirts, appealing though that prospect might be. As studies have shown, this chemical element of romance lessens over time. One researcher has found that the altered brain chemistry of falling in love lasts roughly six to eight months. Others have found that it takes two to three years for the feelings of infatuation to fade to feelings of neutrality—not mild attraction but neutrality!

The problem with relying on our passion to guide us is that a marriage has to stand the test of time to be successful. Some people may feel relieved when they get divorced, but I don't think anyone has ever counted it as a success. To base a long-term relationship on short-term chemistry alone is a little like buying a car based on how it's going to run for the first one hundred miles.

This isn't a marital problem. It's a human problem. We all experience this waning of desire in countless ways. The excitement of anticipation gives way to the dullness of routine. If you have ever bought a new car or started a new job, you have experienced this sensation. This isn't such a big deal when it comes to a car purchase. If you have the money, it's a relatively simple matter to get a new car. But it is a huge deal when it comes to marriage. The funny thing about the waning of our desires is that even though all of us have gone through this multiple times, studies show that we forget about it each and every time. We also do a terrible job of predicting how we will feel in the future, always expecting that it will be more like that present than it is. You can imagine how potentially destructive these habits of mind are for a couple who marries while still infatuated with each other.

If you are one of those people who simply refuse to accept this and want your passion to burn as brightly after forty years as it does after one day, there is one possible solution—more sex. According to several experiments, animals show less habituation to positive feelings when given oxytocin, which is released during sex. It's not clear how much sexual activity it will take to hold habituation at bay, but I invite any energetic readers to give it their best shot. For the rest of us, it's time to come to terms once again with the cost of the romantic story line.

BEWARE EXPECTATIONS, PART II

Perhaps the biggest single problem for many married couples today is the enormous expectations that are routinely loaded onto marriage by both the culture at large and the couples themselves. Just think of the various social roles that have been conflated into the marital relationship—best friend, closest kin relationship, sexual playmate, and economic partner to name just a few. So many extravagant hopes are now built into marriage that some researchers have dubbed it "the cult of the couple"—a cult that can even prove fatal. According to research, men who murder their wives are especially strong believers in the idea of finding a soul mate and practicing strict monogamy. Traditionally, though, this was not the case. Your wife or husband was just that, and people did not expect their partners to perform numerous other roles, such as best friend.

Of course, traditionally, marriage itself was based on a number of considerations of which love was only one. A whole array of forces—economic, religious, and societal—buttressed the commitment between a man and a woman, but that has changed.

Today, for example, fewer women are having children, and more women are economically independent than ever before. In many ways, that's a wonderful development. But it means that even the economic and parental bonds that used to tie a husband and wife together are disappearing. As these traditional ties disappear, the only thing left holding the relationship together is love, and that is a very fragile reed on which to rest so much weight. With all of those other bonds stripped away, marriage is dependent solely on personal fulfillment—or, to put a fig leaf on it, love. But this shift has only worsened the problem. The more committed we become to the narrow idea that marriage should be the source of most of our happiness, the more dissatisfied we inevitably become with the relationship itself. In the early 1970s, the percentage of men who described their marriage as "very happy" was 70 percent. By the mid-1990s, that number had fallen to 64 percent. Women have experienced the same drop, the number of "very happy" falling from 67 percent to 62 percent. It's no accident that this has occurred at precisely the same time that love has been enshrined as *the* key to marriage.

At the very least, we need to recognize that marriage is not a solution to all of life's problems. In *A General Theory of Love*, the authors declare, "When they do get down to relating, Americans find they have been tutored for years in the wrong art. In a dazzling vote of confidence for form over substance, our culture fawns over the fleetingness of being *in love* while discounting the importance of *loving*." In fact, the relationship itself, for all of its benefits, creates a number of problems all on its own, so much so that one psychologist has called marriage "a disagreement machine." Evolutionary psychology itself provides little comfort for those who would like to believe that a happy marriage is a simple and natural achievement. As David Buss has noted, "Humans were not designed by natural selection to coexist in niceness and matrimonial bliss. They were designed for individual survival and genetic reproduction. The psychological mechanisms fashioned by these ruthless criteria are often selfish ones."

Although a successful marriage does bring all sorts of wonderful benefits, we would all be much more likely to achieve that goal if we lowered our expectations about what marriage will do for us. Actually, you can make the argument that we would be better off if we lowered our expectations across the board. When it comes to life satisfaction, Danes easily outclassed the competition in an international survey. One of the reasons is that they have consistently low expectations for the future. But to return to the question of love, it's not that we shouldn't include it as one of the considerations when we get married. However, love alone is not enough. Perhaps the question is not why almost half of our marriages end in divorce but, given our exalted expectations, how half of them manage to succeed. I hope this chapter can offer some answers to that question.

WHY IT'S BETTER NOT TO BE TOO MUCH IN LOVE

One place we might look for answers is arranged marriages. Earlier, I cited a study of Indian arranged marriages, which found that those marriages were happier over time than Western marriages. Orthodox Jews who use a matchmaker have reported similar experiences of love continuing to grow after marriage. If we are willing to loosen our grip on the romantic story line, we might just find that our ideas about the course of love and marriage are out of whack. Right now, our ideal image of marriage looks something like this:

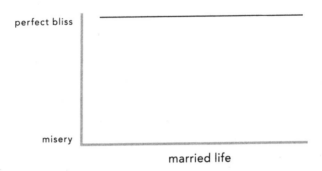

We are supposed to be ecstatic on our wedding day and also live happily ever after. Does that look remotely realistic to anyone? Yet that is the rough outline of most pop culture presentations of the romantic story line. Now, let's look at a graph at what love looks like for arranged marriages:

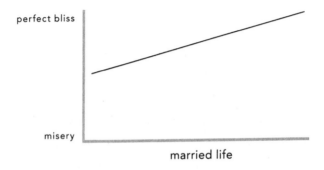

Doesn't that seem both more realistic and, ultimately, a far healthier outlook for long-term happiness?

What I'm saying strikes at the core of the romantic story line and at some of our most cherished myths about love and marriage. But the research is there to back it up. Take, for example, the PAIR Project run by Ted Huston at the University of Texas at Austin. Launched back in 1981, the project has followed 168 newlyweds, studying everything from their early courtship to the eventual success or failure of the relationship. His work is unusually revealing because it looks at couples much earlier in their relationship and for a much longer period of time than virtually any other study. And what Huston and his fellow researchers have discovered challenges many of the central elements of the romantic story line.

Let's start with the idea that you should marry someone you are madly in love with. Who hasn't attended a wedding where the couple seems completely enamored with each other and thought, I hope I find a love like that. It turns out that our envy of those blissful couples is entirely misplaced. They are more likely to get divorced because those feelings of romantic ecstasy are impossible to maintain (less surprisingly, the PAIR project also found that couples who have a brief courtship are more vulnerable to divorce and that many newlyweds are not blissfully in love when they marry).

This is only one of a number of surprising findings. For example, it turns out that even large differences in taste are not important to the success of a marriage — *unless* you brood about them. Brooding, they found, leads to divorce. And conflict itself is not a sign of trouble; instead, the key for couples is to preserve positive feelings for each other. Loss of affection, not conflict, is the great predictor of divorce. Even longevity is not necessarily an indication of success. Huston has found that some couples have lackluster relationships but do not divorce. They basically accept that married life is a source of modest dissatisfaction.

The PAIR project does offer support for some folk wisdom. For example, women should trust their intuition. Women in the study who feared that the marriage might have future problems generally discovered that their fears were well founded. You also don't have to hang around for years to see if the marriage will improve. According to Huston, the first two years tend to reveal whether or not you are going to be happy. And forget about having a baby to solve your problems. The birth of a child does not change how a couple feels about each other. The project also confirms what numerous other studies have suggested—men with feminine traits make better husbands.

I know what you are thinking. You would never fall into any of these traps. You are too savvy. You probably feel that you can just look at a couple and predict with great accuracy whether or not they will stay together. Well, I'm here to tell you that you are deluded, at least according to a study by Rachel Ebling and Robert Levenson. The two researchers showed people three-minute videotapes of five couples who stayed married and five couples who got divorced and then asked the viewers to make predictions about those couples. Most people were terrible at predicting which couples would get divorced and scored at a level only 4 percent above random chance. In this instance, women's intuition also proved to be no help. The study found that women were no better at predicting than men. And in a stunning confirmation of body language over spoken language, the researchers found that listening to the actual content of the conversations made for less accurate predictions. But the scary part is what Ebling and Levenson found when they gave the same test to trained professionals, such as therapists. It turned out that the pros were just as bad at figuring out what would happen to the couples as the ordinary people and scored no better than if they had randomly guessed.

Married couples who are feeling smug about how well they know their partners should also take stock. According to another study, the longer couples were married to each other, the worse they became at reading each other's minds. They also became more confident over time in their ability to guess what their partner was thinking. In other words, they were getting more confident in their predictions at the same time that their predictions were getting less accurate. The reason for this failure of marital communication was that the longer a couple was married, the less attention they paid to each other. For any theory of marriage predicated on good communication, the study reveals just how daunting that task can be.

THE LOVE LAB

While you or I may not be very good at predicting whether or not a couple has the right stuff or even what our partner is thinking, there is someone who is very good at it—John Gottman, a psychologist at the University of Washington. He runs the Gottman Institute, which has been affectionately dubbed "the love lab."

Gottman has been studying couples and trying to understand why they succeed and fail since the 1970s. To do this, he has come up with a method of analysis that is probably the most rigorous attempt to decode marital interactions ever invented. Typically, he will videotape a couple while they discuss something about which they disagree. That in itself is nothing special. What sets Gottman apart is his method of analysis. He and his researchers then break down the tape for both content and affect. He has developed an elaborate scoring system that covers virtually every emotion a couple might express. Each fleeting emotional tic is scored so that a few seconds' exchange will result in several notations for each person. The love lab also adds another layer of data—the couples are hooked up to heart monitors as well as other biofeedback equipment to measure people's stress levels during the conversation. To give you some idea of how rigorous and exhaustive this method is, Gottman estimates that it takes twenty-eight hours to analyze a single hour of videotape.

What all this painstaking analysis offers is a level of precision unequalled by anyone else studying marriage. Gottman's methods are incredibly good at determining which couples will succeed and which will fail. How good? If he analyzes an hour-long conversation, he can predict with 95 percent accuracy if a couple will still be married fifteen years later. Needless to say, after years of practice, Gottman has become spectacularly good at seeing what most of us miss. He understands relationships in the way that Tiger Woods plays golf—with a kind of effortless grasp that makes the rest of us look inept.

We can't all be John Gottman, but we can use the insights that he has developed. For those in a relationship who want to know whether their partnership will succeed or fail *right now*, Gottman has outlined a number of patterns that can help reveal whether or not newlyweds will get divorced, which he can identify based on watching the couple for only three minutes. The first crucial element is how the discussion starts. Women usually are the ones to open the conversation (one reason why the words a man most fears to hear are, "We need to talk"), and they establish the tone of the exchange. The question is, does the woman begin with a harsh or a soft opening? That will determine much of what follows. Second, does the woman complain about something specific (I wish you would take the garbage out) or something global and character related (You are so lazy—you can't even bother to take the garbage out). If a couple can master the soft opening and the specific complaint, they will be a long way toward a happy marriage. The partner's reaction to all of this is also crucial. Is he open to his wife's influence? Yes, it's true—listening to your wife is incredibly important for a happy marriage. Does his response amplify over time (in other words, does he stay calm or get angry)? And does he get defensive, which will make him reject his wife's influence and likely get more angry? If the husband tends to get defensive, the couple also has a higher chance of divorce. There—success or failure in three minutes or less.

Unfortunately, even in the cause of scientific inquiry, married couples are reluctant to put their squabbles on display for an importunate author like myself, so I have had to turn to a different source for my marital spats. In contrast to the other chapters, my examples here are not drawn from real life but from literature, and I believe I have discovered an exemplary couple when it comes to illustrating Gottman's principles of communication

Wooster remains impervious to his wife's, I mean his valet's, influence.

JEEVES: Very good, sir.

Jeeves is intelligent enough not to push the argument to any sort of breaking point. After a number of pages of hijinks on the part of Wooster and sagacity on the part of Jeeves, we return again to the tie.

WOOSTER: Jeeves!
JEEVES: Sir?
WOOSTER: That pink tie.
JEEVES: Yes sir?
WOOSTER: Burn it.

Ultimately, Wooster overcomes his defensiveness and accepts Jeeves's influence on the all-important subject of the proper fashionable attire for a gentleman, a model of marital communication that aids their sturdy partnership through many a tight spot.

Besides helping explain the success of certain literary partnerships, Gottman can even give you a rough time frame for when you might get divorced. If a couple has a lot of what he calls negative affect (i.e., nastiness toward each other), they will probably get divorced in the first seven years. But Gottman found that using this metric alone missed many couples who later divorced.

So he went back and studied the videotapes again and found that a *lack* of positive affect (being nice to each other) also undermined a marriage. It didn't work as quickly, but around the time the couple's first child reached the age of fourteen, the couples had generally become so emotionally detached that they ended up divorcing.

CAN YOU HEAR ME NOW?

Gottman's fine-grained analysis has revolutionized our understanding of how and why relationships work or don't work. In the first place, many of the traditional techniques of marital therapy have turned out to be completely ineffective. In fact, unhappy couples who had undergone therapy fell back into their dysfunctional ways at such a high rate that many considered it a crisis for the profession. To give you one example, let's look at an approach known as active listening. This technique became so popular for a while that you didn't just come across it in marital counseling. You were probably taught some version of it if you participated in any kind of workshop having to do with conflict resolution. Active listening involves the listener constantly checking to see if he or she has correctly understood the speaker, usually by paraphrasing and repeating what the speaker has said. The theory is that you are forced to listen and understand first, rather than respond, which—if the theory were correct—would foster understanding and communication and help defuse defensiveness. As you might imagine, this leads to incredibly stilted conversations. Here is how a typical active listening exchange might develop:

JOHN: I'm really angry that you were late tonight.

LISA: I hear what you are saying. You are angry with me for being late.

JOHN: Yeah, you never show up on time! It's like my own time doesn't matter.

LISA: You feel like I don't value your time as much as my own.

Etc.

Gottman decided to put active listening to the test in his lab. The first thing he found was that happy couples don't use anything remotely like active listening, and the vast majority of couples who had been trained to use it didn't find that their problems were lessened. A small group did manage to adopt the techniques with some success, but follow-up studies showed that all of those couples had relapsed into their old habits within a year.

He also looked at another therapeutic technique that is probably most accurately described as the quid pro quo method. As you might expect, this approach involves responding to your partner in a tit-for-tat fashion. If your partner does something nice for you, you are supposed to do something nice back. When Gottman looked at this method, the news was even worse: the quid pro quo approach actually harmed the relationship. People generally get a warm feeling when they do something nice for someone else, but couples using the quid pro quo method found that they could no longer take pleasure in giving because it had become part of an explicit exchange and, thus, no longer felt like giving at all. It turns out that married couples should follow the wisdom of Jack Kennedy's first inaugural speech and ask not what your spouse can do for you but what you can do for your spouse.

WHY FIGHTING IS LIKE DEATH AND TAXES

The good news is that Gottman has also identified what does work in a marriage. Let's start by dismissing one item that many couples think is important but that actually isn't: fighting. The common myth of the romantic story line is that happy couples don't fight, but Gottman has found that fighting is not a predictor of divorce. Happy couples fight just as much as unhappy couples. While it is true that some couples rarely argue, this is probably a sign of poor communication, not of marital bliss. Arguing regularly is healthier than never fighting, so couples who fight less are also less satisfied over time. The problem for non-fighting couples is that, by never fighting, they let things build up too much—*way* too much. Couples with serious problems wait an average of six years before they seek professional help, and six years is a lot of bad juju to try to undo.

What this means is that conflict and disagreement are an inescapable part of marriage. Just how inescapable? Gottman has found that most of the subjects married couples disagree about are *never* resolved. That's right. NEVER. From his examination of thousands of couples, he has discovered that 69 percent of them never resolve their conflicts. So, if you ever have the feeling that you are caught in some bizarre version of *Waiting for Godot* and are having the same argument yet again, you're probably right.

Most couples fight about the same things as well (typically money, the division of labor, and children), so we are all caught in the same version of *Waiting for Godot*. The good news is that a failure to resolve conflicts is not a sign of marital failure.

What matters is not whether you fight but *how* you fight, and once again, marital therapists had been peddling snake oil to an unsuspecting public. Traditionally, in a therapist's office, conflict is dealt with forthrightly and unrelentingly. When one person gets uncomfortable and wants to change the subject, he or she is forced to stay the course and keep slogging through the argument, which may be a useful way to run a meeting in a corporation but is a disaster for a marriage. Gottman found that happy couples didn't follow this method and disrupted their arguments in all sorts of ways. They told jokes or went off on irrelevant tangents for a while (they also didn't escalate the argument; "Pick up your clothes" never became "you're a bad person"). They did all sorts of things while they were arguing that many marital therapists would put a stop to. But it turns out that there are some very good reasons for changing the subject. Remember all those sensors that Gottman attached to couples in the love lab? He was measuring their physiological response during the conversation, and what he discovered was that our ability to argue is dependent on our ability to remain calm. Once the argument starts to get heated, and the person's heart rate goes above one hundred, that person loses the ability to argue in a reasonable fashion. In effect, the body goes on tilt and swamps the person's ability to be rational. So, all those conversational dodges that happy couples resort to when they are disagreeing serve a useful purpose—they give the couples a chance to catch their breaths and to keep their bodies from rocketing past the physio-logical breaking point.

Gottman also found something else that will come as a sur-prise to those who view women as the more emotional sex. Dur-ing arguments, men are much more likely to be overwhelmed by their physiological response, to become, in Gottman's words, "flooded." That helps explain why men are more likely to avoid getting into an argument with their wives and to engage in what Gottman calls stonewalling—they simply can't handle their body's physical response to an argument. They know that their blood pressure will ratchet up, and their heart will start pound-ing, and they will lose it. So, in the classic choice of fight or flight, they choose flight. Because of this, the burden of raising these issues is on women. Gottman has found that more than 80 percent of the time, the wife is the one who brings up difficult issues. And that's true of the happy marriages as well.

Perhaps most important, happy couples manage to main-tain a remarkably high level of positive to negative comments—fully five to one—even when they are fighting! The contrast with failing relationships couldn't be more stark. Unhappy couples generally don't even achieve a ratio of one to one (averaging roughly 0.8 positive comments to every one negative comment). That sounds impossible. How do couples maintain a positive ratio during the fight itself? The key is that happy couples never go for broke in an argument. They never find themselves in that fatal position when each partner is simply trying to wound the other because of how angry he or she is. A woman in a happy couple will say, "I appreciate how hard you work at the office, but I still think I deserve more help at home," rather than

"You never help me at home, and you don't even make enough money so that we can afford a cleaning lady." So, the key for a married couple is not to avoid fighting but simply to fight well, abiding by a marital version of the Marquee de Queensbury rules.

To look at the ways unhappy couples go wrong, let's take another representative couple from literature, Martha and George from Edward Albee's *Who's Afraid of Virginia Woolf?*

> MARTHA: I don't know what you're so tired about . . . you haven't *done* anything all day; you didn't have any classes, or anything. . . .

Notice the harsh opening. She doesn't just ignore his previous complaint about being tired. She argues that his complaint is without any legitimacy and then turns it into a criticism of him for not being more active.

> GEORGE: Well, I'm tired . . . If your father didn't set up these goddamn Saturday night orgies all the time . . .

George is defensive. Rather than respond to her remarks, he opens up a new line of attack about her father and about the life her father forces them to lead.

> MARTHA: Well, that's too bad about you, George . . .

A line dripping with sarcasm and filled with contempt for George's inability to be more vital.

GEORGE (crumbling): Well, that's how it is, anyway.

A defensive repetition.

MARTHA: You didn't *do* anything; you never *do* anything; you never *mix*. You just sit around and *talk*.

She heightens the conflict, moving to a general character assassination. Whereas she complained a few lines earlier that he didn't do anything all day, now she complains that he never does anything.

GEORGE: What do you want me to do? Do you want me to act like you? Do you want me to go around all night *braying* at everybody the way you do?

This leads not just to more defensiveness but to his own contempt and sarcasm. Although more restrained, his choice of the word bray with its connotations of being loud and uncouth is designed to wound.

MARTHA (BRAYING): I DON'T BRAY!

And it has the desired effect—driving Martha to a mini-tantrum.

A textbook example of how *not* to fight.

WHAT TO AVOID—AND WHAT TO DO

If you do want to look for signs of divorce, don't focus your attention on fighting; instead, focus on the emotions you express toward each other. If either partner regularly expresses negative, judgmental emotions, that is a clear warning sign that a marriage is headed for failure. Gottman narrows it down even more and argues that the real culprits are four key emotions, what he calls the four horsemen of the apocalypse. The first is criticism. But Gottman is only interested in a certain kind of criticism. Concrete criticisms about a specific behavior are fine, but criticisms that attack someone's character are not. The other three emotions to watch for are defensiveness, contempt, and stonewalling. As you might expect, most stonewallers are husbands—85 percent—and this type of behavior is particularly destructive because emotional distance, rather than conflict, is usually what determines whether a marriage will succeed or not. If couples can't fight in a way that doesn't overwhelm the husband emotionally, he is likely to resort to stonewalling. There is one final relationship killer to add to the mix: repairing. During and after fights, happy couples often make attempts to repair the damage. Unhappy couples also make those attempts. The problem is that they usually fail. Either the other person rejects them, or the repair comes with a sting attached. If couples have unleashed the four horsemen and are failures at repairing, that is a guaranteed recipe for divorce. If all of this is a little complicated to keep track of, Gottman has a simpler method: ask a couple about their marital history. He found that if the couple has a positive memory of their life together, they are very likely to have a happy future as well (94 percent likely—not too shabby).

Besides avoiding the four horsemen, there are several things that couples can do to improve their marital happiness. The first is simply to pay better attention to your spouse. According to Gottman, there are key moments every day when your partner asks for your interest in something, and you can either respond positively or not. Although these are generally small matters (a discussion of what to eat for dinner or a problem at work), they can quickly become a pattern of behavior so that couples either regularly show interest in each other or consistently ignore each other. You would be surprised by how little time it can take over the course of the week to develop this pattern. And husbands really do need to listen to their wives. Happier marriages generally have men who are willing to accept the influence of their spouses. Couples also have to be good at calming each other down so that arguments don't rage out of control. There is even a division of labor when it comes to marital arguments. Husbands are usually the ones who de-escalate a low-intensity conflict, while wives are the ones who de-escalate a high-intensity conflict.

None of these are necessarily large changes, and that is one of the heartening findings of Gottman's research. Turning a marriage around doesn't require whole-scale reinvention. It requires lots of small things done on a regular basis. What causes trouble is the very dailyness of marriage. The petty squabbles and minor annoyances that act like a form of Chinese water torture. Any one individual incident is not necessarily that significant, but when you add them all up, they can become overwhelming. If you can turn those routine interactions around—so that, for example, a couple learns to laugh a little bit when they argue—then those daily interaction start working to reinforce, rather than undermine, the marriage.

KNOW THYSELF—EXCEPT WHEN IT COMES TO YOUR MARRIAGE

The funny thing is that happy couples don't just succeed because they have mastered these techniques—they also succeed because they cling to an inaccurately rosy view of their partner and of their married life. That's right. Happy couples seem to engage in a certain amount of what could be called healthy self-deception. This is so common that psychologists have even coined a term for it, "marital aggrandizement." For example, one study revealed that some spouses assume a greater level of similarity than actually exists and that the assumed level of similarity is a better indicator for marital satisfaction than the actual level of similarity. So, happy couples aren't necessarily more similar than unhappy couples, but the more that couples perceive themselves to be similar, the happier they are likely to be.

Offering some confirmation that husbands may be more like Homer Simpson than any of us want to imagine, wives are particularly adept at this mental trick. In one study, wives used a kind of perceptual filter to evaluate their husband's behavior. In a happy marriage, wives judged an interaction with their husbands as pleasurable when an objective observer only saw it as neutral. This kind of consistent perceptual shift can go a long way to keeping a wife satisfied with her husband. It can also work the opposite way in an unhappy marriage so that wives judge everything more harshly.

Self-deception is a useful trick when it comes to any nagging doubts about the relationship. In a study on marital conviction, the researchers found that a strong sense of conviction in the marriage depended on having no significant doubts, and that avoiding those doubts involved self-deception. The more satisfied couples tend to be with each other, the more they tend to idealize one another, although you can't simply lie to yourself. The study showed that there has to be an element of truth to the claim. That said, there are a variety of strategies couples use to inflate their views of each other. One is simply to convince yourself that the qualities your partner has are the qualities you always wanted. Another strategy is to downplay faults by tying them to virtues (my husband may work more than I want, but that is because he is a good provider). A key part of the equation turns out to be a healthy amount of self-esteem. Without it, the researchers found that people have more difficulty idealizing their partners and also underestimate how their partners feel about them, so your doubts about your relationship may in fact be doubts about yourself. Regardless, when it comes to marriage, the research suggests that rose-colored glasses are a necessary accessory.

And if you love your spouse but wish you could change one thing about them, I have some paradoxical advice: You should treat them as if they already embody the quality you wish they had. That may seem a strange way to get what you want, but studies show that people want to live up to the positive image that other people have of them, while complaining generally only results in defensiveness.

Beyond that, I'm afraid there are no simple answers. To misquote Tolstoy, I used to believe that all happy marriages were happy in the same way. But I was wrong. It turns out that there are many successful variations, and a relationship can never be reduced to a formula. Even if it could, no marriage remains static over a lifetime. If you hang in there long enough, though, you may even outlast some of the problems endemic to relationships. For example, as men age, studies show that they care less about sexual variety, and other studies have found that "old" love is even more satisfying than "young" love. If all of this is vague and unsatisfying, I can offer one quick and easy tip for staying together: have a boy. Studies show that having a son decreases the likelihood of divorce. Beyond that, all I can say is learn to fight fair.

I will end with one final study that I find strangely comforting. Married couples really do grow to look more alike over time, apparently because they tend to mirror each other's facial expressions and, thus, make similar use of the underlying facial muscles. If we can share enough happy moments as a couple, that sounds like an appealing fate.

Epilogue

AFTER ALL MY RESEARCH, MY FAVORITE PIECE OF WISDOM comes not from science but from the last lines of *Annie Hall*. I'll let Woody Allen tell his own joke:

After that it got pretty late, and we both had to go, but it was great seeing Annie again. I realized what a terrific person she was, and how much fun it was just knowing her; and I thought of that old joke, you know, this guy goes to a psychiatrist and says, "Doc, my brother's crazy. He thinks he's a chicken." And the doctor says, "Well, why don't you turn him in?" The guy says, "I would, but I need the eggs." Well, I guess that's pretty much now how I feel about relationships. You know, they're totally irrational, and crazy, and absurd, but I guess we keep going through it because most of us need the eggs.

Even with the latest research, there remains something unknowable about love. Why do you choose one person rather than another? Why do two people fall out of love? Or remain happily married? Scientists' incomplete answers to the fundamental questions of attraction teach us an important lesson about our own love lives. Love is endlessly elusive, not a final result but an achievement, one that requires a daily attempt to throw a rope across the chasm that separates us from each other. Perhaps the most that all of this scientific research can do is help us understand our experiences in ways that will improve our chances of finding love and give us the equanimity to bear the inevitable disappointments that will come along the way.

Although I have tried to knock the romantic story line off its pedestal, I never wanted to suggest that we remove it entirely from our lives, because the best lives, the happiest lives, are those that approach life not as a tragedy or as a farce but as a romance. Even with all the difficulties of romance in the modern world, each of us can name inspiring stories of love that really did conquer all. Childhood sweethearts who are as in love at eighty as they were at eighteen. Long-lost love that burns just as brightly when the lovers are finally reunited. I even spoke to one couple who went through a painful divorce only to fall in love again years later and remarry, a testament to the possibility of finding love in the most unlikely places. As E. M. Forster wrote in the epigraph to *Howard's End*, "Only connect," which serves as useful advice not just in our search for love but in the most basic expression of our humanity.

Acknowledgments

WRITING A BOOK IS A LITTLE LIKE A LONG-TERM RELATION-ship that comes to an end. It begins with great enthusiasm. There are periods in the middle when you find yourself wondering what you are doing and worrying that you have made a terrible mistake. It usually goes on far too long. And when it's finally over, you look back and try to remember what happened.

With that said, I owe a debt to many people who helped me hang in there and see the relationship through to its end. I want to thank Judith Riven, my agent, for reacting with excitement to my initial idea, even though the more usual response might have been an attempt to dissuade me from ranging so far afield. I also want to thank my editor, Lucia Watson, and my publisher, Megan Newman, who were enthusiastic about this project right from the start. In addition, I want to express my gratitude to the rest of the team at Avery who all did an outstanding job.

I am enormously grateful to the New York Public Library, particularly for librarian extraordinaire David Smith. The library's collections and its generosity in providing work space made this book possible. I also am indebted to the many men and women who were kind enough to share their experiences with me.

And since our parents play a key role in shaping most of our ideas about relationships, I would like to thank my own for planting the seeds, directly and indirectly, for *Decoding Love*. My mother passed along her interest in relationships, and my father taught me to question the things we assume we know. He deserves an extra thanks for providing the inspiration for *Decoding Love* by giving me a book about economics. It gives me great pleasure to think that this is probably the first book on attraction ever inspired by the dismal science.

Most of all, I want to thank my wife, Heesun, for being so supportive throughout the inevitable vicissitudes of writing a book, despite her being busy with the trials of pregnancy. She was too kind to point out which gestation was more difficult.

(December, 1988): 485–496. For the problems caused by thinking too much about which painting to choose, see T. D. Wilson, et al., "Introspecting about reasons can reduce post-choice satisfaction," *Personality and Social Psychology Bulletin* 19:3 (June, 1993): 331–339. For the difficulties of too many jams, see T. D. Wilson and J. W. Schooler, "Thinking too much: Introspection can reduce the quality of preferences and decisions," *Journal of Personality and Social Psychology* 60:2 (February, 1991): 181–192. For the power of introspection to change our views about our romantic relationships, see T. D. Wilson and D. Kraft, "Why do I love thee?: Effects of repeated introspections about dating relationships on attitudes toward the relationship," *Personality and Social Psychology Bulletin* 19:4 (August, 1993): 409–418. For the ability of teacher expectations to transform student achievement, see R. Rosenthal and L. Jacobson, *Pygmalion in the Classroom: Teacher expectation and pupil's intellectual development* (Williston, VT: Crown House Publishing, 2003). For the probing study of colonoscopies and Kahneman's peak-end rule, see D. A. Redelmeier and D. Kahneman, "Patients' memories of painful medical treatments: real-time and retrospective evaluations of two minimally invasive procedures" in *Pain* 66:1 (1996): 3–8. For the study on "North Dakotan" wine, see Brian Wansink, et al., "Fine as North Dakota wine: Sensory experiences and food intake," in *Physiology and Behavior* 90:5 (2007): 712–716. For the power of an attractive woman's picture to change the nature of a telephone conversation, see M. Snyder, et al., "Social perception and impersonal behavior: On the self-fulfilling nature of social stereotypes," *Journal of Social Psychiatry* 35 (1977): 656–666. For one of the many studies on lottery winners and accident victims, see P. Brickman, D. Coates, and R. Janoff-Bulman, "Lottery winners and accident victims: Is happiness relative?" *Journal of Personality and Social Psychology* 36:8 (August, 1978): 917–928.

For those interested in the Darwinian perspective, David Buss's *The Evolution of Desire: Strategies of Human Mating* (New York: Basic Books, 2003) is a fascinating account of evolutionary psychology and relationships (in fact, all of his books make excellent reading). Matt Ridley's *The Red Queen: Sex and the Evolution of Human Nature* (New York: Harper Perennial, 2003) is an insightful look at the never-ending battle simply to stay in place, and Donald Symons's *The Evolution of Human Sexuality* (Oxford: Oxford University Press, 1979), though sadly out of print, will astound the most jaded reader. For discussions of chimps, bonobos, and humans, see the collection of essays, *Tree of Origin: What primate behavior can tell us about human social evolution* (Cambridge: Harvard University Press, 2001). For a comparison of the speed of primate coitus, see Desmond Morris's *The Naked Ape* (New York: McGraw-Hill, 1967). For an extended study of the evolution of pair-bonding, see Helen Fisher's *The Sex Contract* (New York: William Morrow Publishing, 1982). R. L. Trivers's famous essay can be found in *Sexual Selection and the Descent of Man: The Darwinian Pivot* (Piscataway, NJ: Transaction Publishers, 2006) edited by B. Campbell. For the willingness of men to have sex with strangers (and vice versa for women), see R. D. Clark and E. Hatfield, "Gender differences in receptivity to sexual offers," *Journal of Psychiatry and Human Sexuality* 2:1 (1989): 39–55. For the differences between male and female fantasies, see D. Symons and B. Ellis, "Sex differences in sexual fantasy: An evolutionary psychology approach," *Journal of Sex Research* 27:4 (November, 1990): 527–555. For men's interest in their female friends, see A. Bleske and D. Buss, "Can men and women be just friends?" *Personal Relationships* 7:2 (June, 2000): 131–151. For the study on toxic fruit fly sperm, see William Rice, "Sexually antagonistic male adaptation triggered by experimental arrest of female evolution" in *Nature* 381 (May 16, 1996): 232–234. For female orgasm and sperm retention, see R. R. Baker and M. A. Ellis's "Human sperm competition: Ejaculate manipulation by females and a function for the female orgasm," *Animal Behavior* 46 (1993): 887–909. For one of the many studies about our addiction to deception, see Bella M. DePaulo, et al., "Lying in everyday life," *Journal of Personality and Social Psychology* 70:5 (May, 1996): 979–995. For the theory that mating is the driving force in the development of our brains, see Geoffrey Miller's *The Mating Mind: How sexual choice shaped the evolution of human nature* (New York: Doubleday, 2000). For the differences between male and female brains, see Louann Brizendine, *The Female Brain* (New York: Broadway Publishing, 2006). For the many-faceted effect of human attractiveness, see Nancy Ectoff's *Survival of the Prettiest: The science of beauty* (New York: Doubleday, 1999). And for a study on the importance of the waist-to-hip ratio, see D. Singh's "Body Shape and Women's Attractiveness," *Human Nature* 4:3 (September, 1993): 297–321.

For testicle size, penis size, and body dimorphism, see Jared Diamond's *The Third Chimpanzee: The evolution and future of the human animal* (New York: Harper Collins, 1992). For a discussion of the advantages and disadvantages of monogamy and polygamy, see Robert Wright's *The Moral Animal: Why we are the way we are: The new science of evolutionary psychology* (New York: Vintage Books, 1995).

For the indefatigable consumers out there, Barry Schwartz's *The Paradox of Choice: Why More is Less* (New York: Harper Collins, 2004) is a remarkable exploration of the difficulties that too much choice creates for us. The happiness studies I mentioned for chapter 1 also provide a great deal of insight into our ability to make ourselves miserable. For the difficulty of too many jams, see S. Iyengar and M. Lepper, "When Choice is Demotivating: Can

>ity

one desire too much of a good thing?" *Journal of Personality and Social Psychology* 79:6 (December, 2000): 995–1006. For the study on doctors' difficulties when faced with multiple treatments, see D. A. Redelmeier and E. Shafir, "Medical decision making in situations that offer multiple alternatives," *Journal of the American Medical Association* 273:4 (January, 1995): 302–305. For the indecisive photography students, see D. T. Gilbert and J. E. J. Ebert, "Decisions and Revisions: The affective forecasting of changeable outcomes," *Journal of Personality and Social Psychology* 82:4 (April 2002): 503–514. For a study on how people prefer more relative income rather than absolute income compared to their neighbors, see S. Solnick and D. Hemenway, "Is more always better?: A survey of positional concerns," *Journal of Economic Behavior and Organisation* 37 (1998): 373–383. For a discussion of the uses of the Madonna-whore dichotomy, see Symons's *The Evolution of Human Sexuality* (New York: Oxford University Press, 1981). For a full breakdown of sex ratios and their implications for society, see M. Guttentag and P. Secord, *Too Many Women?: The sex ratio question* (Thousand Oaks, CA: Sage Publications, 1983). For a full account of health statistics associated with marriage, see L. Waite and M. Gallagher, *The Case for Marriage: Why married people are happier, healthier, and better off financially* (New York: Doubleday, 2000).

For game theorists and economists, I'm afraid that most of this material is from scholarly sources that have not made it out into the world in a more accessible book form. Perhaps some enterprising readers will be inspired to do it for themselves and make my book obsolete. For the study of what men and women look for, based on lonely hearts' ads, see D. Waynforth and R. Dunbar, "Conditional mate choice strategies in humans: Evidence from 'Lonely Hearts' advertisements," *Behaviour* 132 (1995): 755–779. For one of the studies on what qualities people pay up for, see N. Li, et al., "The necessities and luxuries of mate preference: Testing the trade-offs, *Journal of Personality and Social Psychology* 82:6 (June, 2002): 947–955. For how much men must earn to overcome a height disadvantage and other economic figures for dating, see G. Hitsch, A. Hortacsu, and D. Ariely, "What makes you click: An empirical analysis of online dating," available at www.aeaweb.org/annual_mtg_papers. For an excellent discussion of the benefits and drawbacks of various physical traits, see Steven Landsburg, *More Sex Is Safer Sex: The unconventional wisdom of economics* (New York: Free Press, 2007). For the study showing that women shy away from choosing both the most attractive and the most financially successful men, see S. Chu, et al., "Too good to be 'true'?: The handicap of high-socioeconomic status in attractive males," *Personality and Individual Differences* 42:7 (May, 2007): 1291–1300. For a full exploration of tit for tat, see Robert Axelrod, *The Evolution of Cooperation* (New York: Basic

Books, 1984). For the dowry game, see Peter F. Todd and Geoffrey F. Miller, "From Pride and Prejudice to Persuasion: Satisficing in Mate Search," in *Simple Heuristics That Makes Us Smart* (New York: Oxford University Press, 1999). For the dollar auction, see Martin Shubik, "The Dollar Auction Game: A paradox in noncooperative behavior and escalation," *Journal of Conflict Resolution* 15:1 (March, 1971): 109–114. For Laszlo Mero's discussion of dollar auctions, see his book *Moral Calculations: Game theory, logic and human frailty* (New York: Springer, 1998).

For those on the prowl, I recommend Timothy Perper's *Sex Signals: The Biology of Love* (Philadelphia: Isi Press, 1986) and David Givens's *Love Signals: A Practical Field Guide to the Body Language of Courtship* (New York: St. Martin's Press, 2004). For the lap dance study, see G. Miller, J. M. Tybur, and B. D. Jordan, "Ovulatory cycle effects on tip earnings by lap dancers: Economic evidence for human estrus?" *Evolution and Human Behavior* 28:6 (November, 2007): 375–381. For the power of eye contact, see D. Walsh and J. Hewitt, "Giving men the come-on: The effect of eye contact and smiling in a bar environment," *Perceptual and Motor Skills* (December, 1985): 873–874. For a female's fifty-two nonverbal signals for attracting a man's attention, see Monica Moore, "Nonverbal courtship patterns in women: Context and consequences," *Ethology and Sociobiology* 6:4 (1985): 237–247. For the different approaches to seduction, based on essays by men and women, see Perper, *Sex Signals*. For the affective shift that occurs after sex, see D. Buss and M. Haselton, "The affective shift hypothesis: The functions of emotional change following sexual intercourse," *Personal Relationships* 8:4 (December, 2001): 1357–1369. For a historical overview of the changing rankings of what men and women want in a partner, see D. Buss, et al., "A half century of mate preferences: The cultural evolution of values," *Journal of Marriage and Family Life* 63:2 (May, 2001): 491–504. For an analysis of humor's effect on attractiveness, see S. B. Kaufman, et al., "The role of creativity and humor in mate selection" in *Mating Intelligence: Sex, relationships, and the mind's reproductive system*, edited by Glenn Gehr and Geoffrey Miller (Philadelphia: Lawrence Erlbaum Associates, 2007). For how dopamine levels in rats decrease with each sexual encounter, see D. F. Fiorino, et al., "Dynamic changes in nucleus accumbens dopamine efflux during the Coolidge effect in male rats," *Journal of Neuroscience* 17 (June, 1997): 4849–4855. For those interested in the brain in love, I recommend Helen Fisher's *Why We Love: The nature and chemistry of romantic love* (New York: Henry Holt, 2004). For the groundbreaking study on smell, see C. Wedekind, et al., "MHC-dependent mate preferences in humans," *Proceedings of the Royal Society of London* B, 260 (1995): 245–249. For women's preference of creativity over wealth at peak fertility, see M. Haselton and G. Miller, "Women's fertility across the cycle increases short-term attractiveness of creative intelligence," *Human Nature* 17:1 (March, 2006): 50–73. For one study on men's smell preference for women nearing their peak fertility, see R. Thornhill, et al., "Major histocompatibility complex genes, symmetry, body scent attractiveness in men and women," *Behavioral Ecology* 14:5 (September, 2003): 668–678. For the lemon-scented rats, see T. J. Fillion and E. M. Blass, "Infantile experience with suckling odors determines adult sexual behavior in male rats," *Science* 231 (1986): 729–731. For a possible genetic cause to promiscuity, see Edmund Rolls, *The Brain and Emotion* (New York: Oxford University Press, 2000). For a study on prairie voles and vasopressin, see C. Sue Carter, et al., "Physiological substrates of mammalian monogamy: The prairie vole model," *Neuroscience & Biobehavioral Reviews* 19:2 (1995): 303–314.

For marital mavens, I am obviously a big John Gottman fan. He has written several accessible books, including Gottman, et al., *Ten Lessons to Transform Your Marriage: America's Love Lab Experts Share Their Strategies for Strengthening Your Relationship* (New York: Crown, 2006) and Gottman and Nan Silver, *The Seven Principles for Making Marriage Work: A Practical Guide from America's Foremost Relationship Expert* (New York: Crown, 1999). Ted Huston's PAIR project can be found on the web at http://www.utexas .edu/research/pair/ourresearch/index.html. For our general ineptitude at judging marital satisfaction, see R. Ebling and R. Levenson, "Who are the marital experts?" *Journal of Marriage and Family* 65:1 (February, 2003): 130–142. For the benefits of perceiving one's partner as better than he or she is, see S. Murray, "The quest for conviction: Motivated cognition in romantic relationships," *Psychological Inquiry* 10:1 (1999), 23–33. For the value of wearing rose-colored glasses when viewing one's husband, see M. Hawkins, et al., "Marital sentiment override: Does it influence couples' perceptions?" *Journal of Marriage and Family* 64:1 (February, 2002): 193–201. For the tendency of partners to look more like each other over time, see R. B. Zajonc, et al., "Convergence in the physical appearance of spouses," *Motivation and Emotion* 11:4 (December, 1987): 335–346.

This list includes only a few general overviews and the studies that receive more in-depth exploration in *Decoding Love*. I have left out a great deal of outstanding work, much of it appearing as articles in scholarly journals. In all honesty, I have been a pygmy standing on the shoulders of giants, and I have greatly appreciated the boost.

Index

happiness
abundance of choices and, 100–105
in adulterous marriages, 55–56
in arranged marriages, 104–5, 225–27
durability of, 30–32
income and, 115
life satisfaction from marriage,
125–26, 219–20
marital, decline in, 222, 224–25
in marriage, to improve, 241–45
in romantic story line, 30
satisficers vs. maximizers, 105
set point, 32
similarities between partners and,
206, 207
smiles, 69–70
Haselton, Martie, 195
health. See genetic fitness indicators
height
attractiveness of, 212
as genetic fitness indicator, 84–85
market value, 143–45
as predictor of intelligence, 144
societal advantages, 143–44
high-cost signals, 78–79, 154
How Much Would You Pay For a Dollar
game, 162–66
hugs, 208
humor, 183–84, 206
Huston, Ted, 227–28

infidelity
evolutionary basis, 57–58
female orgasm and, 61
genetic profile and, 192
lies about, 65
prevalence of, 55–56
women's sexual fantasies and, 66
See also promiscuity
intelligence
adolescent height as predictor of, 144
attractiveness of, 183, 215
as heritable trait, 72, 145
as hindrance for women, 114, 117
mistaken assumptions and, 55
sexual selection for, 72
Internet dating
abundance of choices, 99

chance of mismatch, 138
criteria, 138–39
lies, 99–100, 155
matching systems, 139–42
values and standards, 100, 153, 155
intuition
ability of animals, 40
overanalysis and, 24, 30
women's superiority at, 76–77, 228
Ismael the Bloodthirsty, 46

"Jeeves and the Unbidden Guest"
(Wodehouse), 232–33
Journal of Consumer Research, The, 18–19

Kahneman, Daniel, 26
Klein, Stefan, 186

language
evolution of, 71–72
in marital communication, 230–34
verbalization, confusion and, 22
women's facility for, 74
See also body language
Levenson, Robert, 228–29
lies. See deception
life expectancy, 48, 125
likability, 205–6
lips, 79, 214
long-term mating. See marriage
love
cultural importance of, 4, 181, 224
fading of, 102, 221–22
growth of, 104, 226
mathematical quantification of, 133
neurochemistry of, 76, 185–86
obstacles, 207
priming, 11–15
romantic story line, 2, 4, 15, 30, 77,
166, 169, 226–27
satisficers vs. maximizers, 105
similar sexual past and, 207
at time of marriage, 227

Machiavellian intelligence theory, 70–72
Madonna-whore dichotomy, 109–12
"Magical Number Seven, The" (Miller),
133